The Smart Woman's Guide to Style & Clothing

A Step-By-Step Process for Creating the Perfect Wardrobe

KARA LANE

ISBN-13: 978-1535071659
ISBN-10: 153507165

Cover image by Tenna Merchent.

Although the author has made every effort to ensure that the information in this book was correct at press time, the author does not assume and hereby disclaims any liability to any party for any loss, damage, or disruption caused by errors or omissions, whether such errors or omissions resulted from negligence, accident, or any other cause.

First Printing, 2016
www.karalane.com

CONTENTS

THE SMART WOMAN'S GUIDE TO
STYLE & CLOTHING

Introduction

- - - - - - - - -

H ave you ever felt like you have too many clothes
but nothing to wear? If so, you are not alone.
According to custom storage company California Closets, the average woman only wears 20 percent
of her clothing. At first, I found that hard to believe.
Then I looked in my closet and realized I wore the same
clothes most of the time and ignored everything else.

We want to look good and feel good in our clothes, but if we are rejecting 80 percent of them, something is clearly not working. To figure out what was going on, I decided to analyze my wardrobe. I counted every item of clothing I owned...tops, pants, jackets, dresses, shoes, handbags, accessories, etc. I was shocked to see I had 604 items, including 41 short-sleeved T-shirts. Who needs 41 short-sleeved T-shirts? Maybe your count would be different, but I bet the number of wardrobe items you own would surprise you.

More important than the actual count are the reasons we are not wearing so many of our clothes. See if any of the following reasons apply to the things you rarely wear:

- Clothes or shoes that do not fit well
- Clothing that does not feel like "you"
- Colors or styles that do not flatter you
- Trendy clothes that are no longer in style
- Shoes or clothes that are not comfortable
- Clothes or shoes that look cheap, frumpy, or worn out
- Fussy clothes with too many buttons, zippers, or embellishments
- Too many clothes for one area of your life and not enough for another
- Assortment of tops, bottoms, and shoes that do not work together as outfits
- Clothes that worked well in the past but do not fit your current body or lifestyle

The clothing we do not wear falls into one of two categories. First are the things we never should have bought, because they never worked for us. Second are the things that once worked for us, but no longer do.

We buy clothes that are not right for us for many reasons: We may buy clothes on impulse. We may not know what looks good on us. We may see something trendy online, in a magazine, or on a celebrity, and buy it because it is currently in style. We may think we are getting a bargain because we bought an item on sale. We may use shopping as retail therapy to improve our mood. We may buy based on habit, purchasing the same type of clothes repeatedly. We may shop when we need something in a hurry, settling for whatever we can find that day. We may shop with friends, who influence our purchases based on their style preferences. We may buy clothes and shoes we think are cute, even if they do not go with anything else in our closet.

In other words, we buy for every reason other than to satisfy our true wants and needs. No wonder we have a closet full of clothes we do not wear! If we were more mindful when shopping, we would only buy wardrobe pieces that fit our lifestyle, flatter our body, and reflect our personal style.

We also hold on to clothes that no longer work for many reasons: We may have gained or lost weight so our clothes no longer fit. We may be reluctant to get rid of items that were expensive. We may have positive memories of when we used to wear the clothes and cannot bear to part with them. We may have gone through a personal change (such as having children) or a professional change (such as switching careers), which affects our clothing needs. We may have just never gotten around to decluttering our closets and drawers.

Whatever the reason, we are holding onto clothing we no longer wear. These items clutter up our closets, making it difficult to get dressed each day because we cannot see what we have. Additionally, looking at clothing we can no longer wear is depressing. It just makes sense to get rid of clothing that no longer serves a useful purpose.

Now that we have discussed the reasons you may have bought or kept clothing that does not work for you, we can begin to talk about what does work. The secret to a perfect wardrobe is versatility, style, and personalization.

To be versatile, your wardrobe must allow you to mix and match clothes and accessories to create many different outfits. A versatile wardrobe allows you to easily transition from casual to dressy, from season to season, and from having too many clothes to having just what you want and need. A versatile wardrobe is simple, functional, and low-maintenance.

To be stylish, your wardrobe must include beautiful pieces that combine classic styles with a modern feel. A stylish wardrobe is timeless, effortless, and chic. It emphasizes quality over quantity. Stylish women do not slavishly follow trends. They wear what looks good on them, fits comfortably, and makes them feel confident.

To be personalized, your clothing must fit your lifestyle, your body, and your personality. No other woman is exactly like you. Your perfect wardrobe is the one that makes you look and feel your best. A personalized wardrobe authentically represents you, rather than turning you into a carbon copy of everyone else. It lets you be you.

While the perfect wardrobe is different for every woman, the principles are the same. To help you achieve your perfect wardrobe, I have created a system that incorporates the principles of versatility, style, and personalization. This process includes step-by-step instructions to help you implement the principles. At the end of the book, I have included a *Style & Clothing Checklist*. The checklist allows you to take the information presented throughout the guide and personalize it to fit you.

If you have read other books on style, you will find this one is a little different. Many style guides are written by fashion designers, fashion journalists, or others in the fashion industry. The books may even be ghost-written by someone else, but credited to a celebrity to sell more books. Having a background in fashion can be helpful, and some books from those in the industry are quite good. However, there are some downsides.

First, some people in fashion have some crazy ideas of style that "real" women like us would never wear. For instance, in a recent spread in *InStyle* magazine, the model wore a leather chap jacket (which consisted of only one sleeve, which was hooked to her neck), a mesh bra top, and a skirt embellished with ostrich plume feathers. Who would actually wear that in public? In fact, who would even wear it in private?

My guide is about wearing clothes that make you look good, not about high fashion avant-garde art.

Second, people in the fashion industry are used to working with high-end designers. As a result, some of their recommendations are beyond the financial means of most women. When I looked at a few fashion magazines recently, I saw a Saint Laurent top in *Marie Claire* for $850, a Miu Miu dress in Vogue for $3,500, and a Giorgio Armani handbag in *Town and Country* for $31,045. Not to mention all the clothing and accessories marked "price upon request." I like many of Nina Garcia's style books, but her recommendations include luxury brands like Manolo Blahnik shoes and Pucci dresses that many women cannot afford.

Before I became an author, I worked in accounting and finance in the insurance industry, so I tend to be financially conservative. Therefore, my recommendations do not include many high-end designer brands. However, I do recommend some "bridge" brands, which are the more affordable lines of clothes, shoes, and handbags from the top designers.

Third, some people in the fashion industry are part of the "fast fashion" trend. Fast fashion is so named because it allows fashion retailers to sell clothes in their stores shortly after the designs appear on the catwalk. That speed comes at a price. It takes time to produce quality garments under ethical factory conditions. That is why fast fashion is sometimes called "throw-away fashion." The clothes are often cheaply priced because they are cheaply made. The fabrics are cheap synthetics and the clothes are poorly constructed. For instance, they may have uneven seams or zippers that stick. The clothes may start falling apart after a couple of washes.

I spent a brief stint as a commercial model (yes, some CPAs can model), and one of the guys on a shoot told me he would just buy shirts at H&M, wear them one time, and throw them away! Getting a top for $10 at fast fashion retailers like H&M, Forever 21, and Zara may seem like a bargain until you factor in how little use you get out of the clothes. Unfortunately, these clothes often end up as part of the 80 percent of clothes you never wear. You can donate them to a nonprofit, but they may end up in landfills or as rags if they are deemed unsalable or unwearable. For all these reasons, I do not recommend cheap brands and stores in this guide.

The fashion industry is just like every other industry. They are in business to make a profit. Fair enough. Just remember that they have a financial incentive to get you to keep buying clothes, shoes, and handbags... whether you need them or not. Buyer beware.

When I was doing my research for this book, I came across a *2015 MarketLine Industry Profile*, which indicated the size of the U.S. womenswear market is over $191 billion. It is forecasted to reach $237 billion by 2019. The U.S. market accounts for 29 percent of the global womenswear market value. That is a lot of clothing, so no wonder we only wear 20 percent of it. You can decide how much you personally want to contribute to increasing the size of the womenswear market.

Through clever marketing and advertising, the fashion industry tempts us with new trends every day. What is "in" one day is "out" the next. If we want to keep up with the trends, we have to keep buying new things...even if the trends do not work for us. However, we do not have to play that game. We can be smart and only buy a trendy new piece if we want it, need it, and it looks good on us. Coincidentally, "smart" has more than one definition. It means intelligent, but it also means sharply dressed. There is no reason why we cannot be both kinds of "smart" and only buy what makes us look and feel good.

Celebrities may be paid to wear designer clothes, but we are not. Smart women ignore the hype and wisely spend money on what they want, not on what retailers want them to buy.

In this guide, I will make recommendations on style and clothing, but you obviously have the final say on what you want to wear. I am not a fashion insider, so I do not benefit from anything you do with your wardrobe. I just want to offer you what I have learned, used, and am passing on to friends...no strings attached. As they say in St. Lucia, "No pressure. No problem."

My wardrobe was a hodgepodge of clothes, shoes, and handbags that I had acquired over time. I wanted a system that would allow me to simplify my wardrobe. I wanted to address issues like color, style, proper fit, putting together outfits, and everything that goes into creating a great wardrobe. I could not find a complete system, so I decided to create one.

I drew on my analytical and organizational skills to develop the *Style & Clothing System* you hold in your hands. I conducted in-depth research on style, studied stylish women, and looked at images on Pinterest,

Polyvore, and various style blogs until I started to see certain patterns. Then I pulled it all together into a process that works for me, and I believe will work for you.

While some style guides are filled with miscellaneous facts, interviews, and general information, this guide includes very specific steps for building your own look-good, feel-good wardrobe. I include clearly defined suggestions, as well as recommending specific brands, stores, and additional style resources.

I will provide you with the tools to create your own versatile, stylish, personalized wardrobe. We will discuss the *Style & Clothing System* I developed, which takes you through the following steps for creating your ideal wardrobe:

Step 1: Identify wardrobe needs based on your lifestyle

Step 2: Select the wardrobe classics that appeal to you

Step 3: Choose your colors, patterns, and clothing styles

Step 4: Know what fits and flatters your body

Step 5: Decide what quality and quantity of clothing you want

Step 6: Pick your shoes, handbags, jewelry, and other accessories

Step 7: Choose your preferred brands and stores

Step 8: Put together outfits and consult style resources as needed

Step 9: Analyze, declutter, and organize your wardrobe

Step 10: Complete your *Style & Clothing Checklist*

The system is clear, complete, and concise. During my research, I discovered why finding the right clothes is more complicated than it seems. For instance, Tim Gunn's *Fashion Bible* mentions that *The Fairchild Dictionary of Fashion* lists 109 different kinds of sleeves, 194 necklines and collars, and 19 different kinds of cuffs! I knew I would have to wade through the data, extract the most important information, and convert it into a process that was simple enough to be useful.

The more I thought about it, the more I realized that finding our style and the clothing that suits us is really a process of elimination. There may be unlimited options, but we do not have to consider all of them. We can narrow down the options to those that work best for us, and then let those options guide our future wardrobe purchases. We do not need to know every possible cut, color, and style of clothing available. We just need to know what fits and flatters us and will not quickly go out of style.

We also do not need to create a different outfit for every single thing we do in our lives. We just need clothing for the *types* of things we do: casual, dressy casual, business, etc. The process becomes simpler over time as we accept some wardrobe options and rule out others.

Having determined that the process could be simplified, my next goal was to create a system that would not be too cookie-cutter. Your style is probably different from my style. The chances that you have the same lifestyle as me, and prefer the same color and style of clothing and accessories as me, and have the same body type and skin tone, and like the same classic wardrobe pieces I do, and are inspired by the same style icons, and…well, you get the point. Each one of us will make different choices for our wardrobes. That originality is part of what defines true style. I designed the *Style & Clothing System* so you could personalize it every step of the way.

Throughout the guide, you will see items marked TIP or CHECKLIST ACTION. TIPs provide additional helpful information. CHECKLIST ACTIONs allow you to personalize the information in each step to suit you.

You will find a *Style & Clothing Checklist* at the end of the book to capture your personal preferences. The checklist will save you time and money when shopping, because it will remind you of your wardrobe wants and needs before you pull out your credit card.

To get the most out of the guide, you may want to read it at least twice. The first time will give you a feel for how the entire process comes together. The second time you can read the guide more slowly and complete the *Style & Clothing Checklist* at the end to capture your personal choices.

If you would like to print off a copy of the *Style & Clothing Checklist*, you can download a copy from my website at http://karalane.com/style-clothing-checklist/.

Be patient in creating your perfect wardrobe. What is perfect for you will change over time based on your personal and financial circumstances. There is no rush. Use what you can from your current wardrobe and build a better one over time. The process is similar to interior design. Just as it takes time to fill your home with things you love, it will take time to fill your wardrobe with things you love.

Above all, remember that true style is about more than how we dress. Who we are and how we treat others matters more than having impeccable taste in clothing.

Furthermore, as Jenni Meyers (the owner of the Beauty + Grace clothing store) notes, "Confidence in a woman is really what makes a woman stylish and beautiful. It isn't really what designer you are wearing; it's about how you love yourself. Confidence is infectious and powerful."

My goal in this guide is to help you feel more confident and beautiful by sharing my *Style & Clothing System*. I want you to look and feel fantastic in your clothes. In the pages that follow are the steps that will help you build your ideal wardrobe. If I have done my job, you will never again have to say, "I have nothing to wear."

BONUS MATERIAL: According to a *New York Times* article, 81 percent of Americans feel they have a book in them. If you have ever thought about writing a book – or are just curious to know how the process works – I have included a behind-the-scenes look at the process I went through to write, publish, and market this book. You will find *Behind the Scenes of The Smart Woman's Guide to Style & Clothing* in the appendix.

Step 1

Identify Wardrobe Needs Based on Your Lifestyle

The first step in the *Style & Clothing System* is to assess your current lifestyle. Where do you live? How do you spend your time? Once you have answered these two questions, you can answer the third: Does your clothing fit your lifestyle?

Our lives change over time, but sometimes our clothes do not. We keep buying the same style of clothing out of habit. Or we buy new clothes for our current activities, but hang on to the old ones as well. We may have moved multiple times and kept packing up our clothing to take with us…even if we never wear it. The older we are, the more likely we have accumulated clothes that no longer fit our lifestyle.

So let's start fresh and talk about your current lifestyle. You can begin by answering the following questions, and then we can identify your wardrobe needs based on your lifestyle.

Where do you live?

The climate where you live affects your wardrobe choices. If you live in a location that is always hot or always cold, you will clearly need fewer clothing options than someone who lives in a seasonal location. I live in a climate where the weather changes significantly between winter, spring, summer, and fall. Temperatures can swing by 100 degrees or more between winter and summer. We also experience more than our fair share of rain, snow, wind, and humidity. Consider the average temperatures and weather conditions in your area.

Your wardrobe needs to account for the weather, but there are ways to make your clothing better serve you. Some clothing and accessories have only one primary function: a winter coat for cold weather, a swim-suit for swimming, and an umbrella for rain. However, you can simplify your wardrobe by choosing versatile pieces whenever possible. For instance, instead of buying a bunch of thick sweaters that can only be worn in winter, you can layer your clothes. In the fall, you can wear a button-down blouse or a cashmere sweater. In the winter, you can layer the sweater over the blouse.

TIP: Layering is also a great option for menopausal women, who may experience extreme hot and cold temperatures regardless of the weather outside!

You can also increase the versatility of your ward-robe by your choice of individual pieces. For instance, a trench coat is a great option for a coat. It provides warmth, protects against rain, and never goes out of style. You can buy a trench coat with a removable liner, allowing you to transition between seasons. Likewise, rather than buying a pair of rain boots, you can water-proof your regular boots or buy weatherproof boots. For example, Aquatalia is an Italian company that makes stylish weatherproof shoes and boots. You can look great wearing them even when it is not raining or snowing.

Additionally, you can choose clothing made of versatile materials to get more use out of your clothing. For instance, pants, jackets, and suits made of gabardine or other seasonless wools can be worn almost year-around.

Finally, you can transition between seasons by mixing clothing from different seasons. For example, as you move from summer to fall, you can wear your summer tops and jeans, but replace your sandals with closed-toe shoes and throw on a denim or leather jacket.

Make your clothes, shoes, and accessories work harder for you. Buy options for your wardrobe that give you greater versatility, such as all-seasons clothing. You will be able to create more outfits with fewer articles of clothing, saving you money and freeing up more closet space.

How do you spend your time?

Take a minute to think about your current lifestyle. First, think about what you do on a daily basis. Do you work? Exercise? Run errands? Raise children? Spend time with your husband or significant other? Hang out at home? Be as specific as possible about the things you do every day.

Second, think about what you do on a weekly basis. Do you have date nights? Lunches with friends?

Dinners out? Movies with family? Social activities? Hobbies or clubs? A church you attend? Chores inside or outside the home?

Third, think about what you do on a monthly basis. Do you volunteer in your community? Attend museums, sporting events, concerts, or other events? Have a girls' night out with your friends?

Finally, think about special occasions in your life that happen less frequently than monthly. Do you travel on vacations? Attend weddings, funerals, parties, fundraisers, black-tie events, or other special ceremonies?

Although the intent of the above questions is to figure out your clothing needs, some people also use the opportunity to reassess their priorities and how they spend their time. That is a good idea, but let's focus on the clothes for now.

Fortunately, you do not need different clothing for every activity and occasion in your life. You really just need clothing suitable for the types of things you do. Unless you have special clothing needs (like maternity clothes), most of your wardrobe needs will likely fall into the following categories, which reflect today's more casual world:

Ultra Casual – to wear at home, in the yard, at the beach, or working out

Casual – to wear in public for errands, lunches, or other informal events

Dressy Casual – to wear for dinner, dancing, or other nicer events or occasions

Dressy – to wear for more formal occasions, like cocktail parties or weddings

Business – to wear to an office, retailer, studio, or wherever you do your work

Feel free to modify the categories or definitions if mine do not work for you. For instance, if you work from home, you may not even need a business wardrobe. If you attend many formal functions, you may need two categories for dressy, possibly cocktail and black tie. What is important is to think in terms of categories. Doing so makes it easier to shop for clothes and put together outfits.

Following are examples of clothing styles for each lifestyle category:

Ultra Casual
- Athletic socks and shoes
- Cotton tank top
- Cut-off denim shorts
- Flip-flops
- Hooded sweatshirt
- Workout clothes
- Yoga pants

Casual
- Blue jeans
- Capris
- Denim skirt
- Fashion sneakers
- Flats
- Polo shirt
- Sandals with low or no heel
- Sundress
- T-shirt
- Turtleneck

Dressy Casual
- Ankle boots
- Black jeans or pants
- Fitted sweater
- Flouncy skirt
- High-heeled sandals or pumps
- Lace top
- Leather leggings
- Party dress
- Silky blouse

Dressy
- Cocktail dress
- Evening gown
- Satin blouse
- Silk pants outfit

- Strappy evening sandals
- Tuxedo jacket
- Velvet skirt

Business

- Blazer
- Dress pants or skirt
- Low-heeled pumps
- Suit
- White blouse

The above list is not all-inclusive, but it should help you visualize the types of clothing you need based on your lifestyle.

You can dress an outfit up or down by simply changing an article of clothing, your shoes, or your accessories. Take jeans as an example. Jeans would normally be considered casual. If you want to dress them down, pair them with something from the ultra casual category, like a tank top or flip-flops. If you want to dress them up, pair them with something from the dressy casual category, like a silky blouse. If you want them to be even dressier, pair them with something from the dressy category, like a tuxedo jacket. If you want them to be more business-like, pair them with something from the business category, like low-heeled pumps. By mixing and matching among categories, you will have a more versatile wardrobe from which to create your outfits.

CHECKLIST ACTION: Rank your wardrobe needs by lifestyle category from most to least important: Ultra Casual, Casual, Dressy Casual, Dressy, and Business. Make a note beside each category of the primary things you do that fall into that category. For instance, dressy casual for you may be clothing needs for date nights, evenings out with friends, and going dancing once a week with your sister.

By focusing on what you need, you will be less likely to buy clothes on impulse that do not fit your lifestyle. Before you buy an article of clothing or pair of shoes, ask yourself, "Where would I wear this?" If it does not fit into your current lifestyle, do not buy it. You will not end up wearing it.

An added benefit of ranking your wardrobe needs is that it helps you discover if you have too many clothes for one area of your life and not enough for another. I am trying to save you from having over 40 casual T-shirts, but nothing to wear on date night. Learn from my mistakes.

Step 2

Select the Wardrobe Classics that Appeal to You

The second step in the *Style & Clothing System* is to familiarize yourself with classic styles of clothing and select the ones you want for your wardrobe. The classics include clothes, shoes, handbags, and other accessories that never go out of style.

The more classics you have in your wardrobe, the less you have to worry about what is currently trending. The classics provide instant, effortless style.

Classics have staying power because they are versatile, well designed, and look good on most women. Some of the classics have been around for a very long time. For instance, the gladiator sandal is over 2,000 years old. It is not likely to go out of style anytime soon. Other classics are newer, such as the wrap dress Diane Von Furstenberg created in 1974.

All the classics have clean lines. You will not find heavily embellished styles or exaggerated shapes among the classics. In other words, you will not find harem pants, culottes, Daisy Duke shorts, jackets with padded shoulders, bell-bottom pants, or overalls on this list. You will find clothing with flattering silhouettes, colors, patterns, and styles.

Keep these classics in mind when you are selecting items for your wardrobe. Regardless of your personal style, you can find classics that will work for you. It is worth investing more in these pieces since you will be able to wear them for a long time to come.

As you read the list of classics, you will notice that some of the pieces specify colors and some do not. That is because sometimes the color is part of what makes the item a classic. After all, the "Little Black Dress" would not be the LBD in any other color.

If you like a classic style but not the color, you have several options. You can buy the style in a different but similar color, such as cream rather than white or midnight blue rather than black. Or you can buy the piece in the classic color and style, but layer something over it. For example, you could wear a colorful jacket over a black turtleneck. Or you can stick with the style, but personalize the look by switching to a completely different color or pattern that better suits you.

> TIP: If you are not familiar with a style from the list below, search on Pinterest or Google Images to see what it looks like.

Classic Clothes

Tops
- Black turtleneck
- Breton striped top
- Cable knit sweater
- Cashmere sweater
- Chambray shirt
- Fair Isle sweater
- Gingham shirt
- Hunter plaid shirt
- Polo shirt

- Silk blouse
- White button-down shirt
- White T-shirt

Pants

- Black jeans
- Black leather pants
- Blue jeans
  (dark, straight-leg jeans are most classic)
- Cigarette pants
- Tailored Bermuda shorts
- Tailored dress pants
- White jeans

Skirts

- A-line skirt
- Pencil skirt

Dresses

- Little black dress (LBD)
- Shift dress
- Shirtdress
- White sheath dress
- Wrap dress

Jackets

- Blazer (black or navy is most classic)
- Denim jacket

- Leather jacket
- Military-inspired jacket
- Safari jacket
- Tuxedo jacket
- Tweed jacket

Suits
- Tailored black pant suit

Coat
- Camel wool coat
- Peacoat (navy is most classic)
- Trench coat (black or tan is most classic)

Swimwear
- Black bikini bathing suit
- Black one-piece swimsuit

Shoes
- Animal-print pumps
- Ankle boots
- Ankle-strap sandals
- Ballet flats
- Black pumps
- Espadrilles
- Gladiator sandals
- Kitten heels
- Knee-high riding boots
- Loafers

- Strappy stilettos
- White sneakers

Handbags
- Clutch purse
- Hobo bag
- Leather tote
- Satchel

Jewelry
- Coral jewelry
- Diamond stud earrings
- Gold or silver hoop earrings
- Gold or silver link necklace
- Metal cuffs
- Pearl necklace
- Tennis bracelet
- Turquoise jewelry

Other Accessories
- Aviator sunglasses
- Wayfarer sunglasses
- Silk scarf

If you are a minimalist, you could build an entire wardrobe made up solely of the classics. The result would be a simple, stylish, versatile wardrobe.

If you want more variety, you can start with the classics that appeal to you. Then, you can add in pieces in additional colors, patterns, and styles to create your perfect wardrobe.

You can also try a modern twist on a classic. Here are a couple of suggestions from Jenni Meyers, owner of the Beauty + Grace clothing store, from an article she wrote called *Closet Classics*:

T-shirt. "A soft tee is a style must! Layer it under a blazer or dress it down with denim. Striped, solids, or inspirational words flash on the front. Grab them when you can and make them the easiest and most affordable way to update your closet."

Sneakers. "Sneakers have come a long way. From your fitness center staple to a fashion statement, no wardrobe is complete without a game-changing pair. Designers have added lace, neon, metallic to your basic tennis shoe making them your new iconic and comfortable must have."

Whatever your personal style, you can find a way to make the classics work for you.

TIP: Purchase the best quality you can comfortably afford. If your clothing budget is tight, you can upgrade to higher quality pieces later. Keep the cost per wear in mind. A $20 top that you only wear twice costs you $10 per wear, and may not look that great. A $60 top that you wear once a month for 5 years costs you $1 per wear, making it a better bargain than the cheaper top.

CHECKLIST ACTION: Make a list of the classics you would like to have.

Step 3

Choose Your Colors, Patterns, and Clothing Styles

— — — — — — — — — — — — — — — — — —

The third step in the *Style & Clothing System* is to select the colors, patterns, and styles of clothing you want for your wardrobe. If you are clear about what you like and find flattering, you can develop your own personal style rather than buying whatever is trendy. I once saw a snarky bumper sticker that said, "You're ugly and your mother dresses you funny." Think of the fashion industry as "your mother," and only listen to her recommendations if they work for you.

You will be able to create a more versatile wardrobe by giving some thought to colors and patterns that work well together. If you instead just grab whatever catches your eye when you are shopping, you will end up with a random assortment of mismatched clothes that you will rarely wear.

The same is true for styles. If you prefer a classic style and buy accordingly, you will end up with tops, pants, skirts, dresses, and shoes that all work together. On the other hand, if you have a confused mixture of preppy, classic, bohemian, glamorous, and romantic styles, you may find it hard to pull together attractive outfits.

So let's figure out your colors, patterns, and styles.

Colors

While there are an almost unlimited number of hues, tints, tones, and shades, listed below are the basic color categories. Without overthinking it, rank these colors from your *most* to *least* favorite:

- Black
- Blue

- Brown
- Gold
- Gray
- Green
- Orange
- Pink
- Purple
- Red
- Silver
- White
- Yellow

Part of looking good in your clothes is feeling good in them. If you like the colors in your wardrobe, you are more likely to feel good in your clothes.

But…there is always a but…*how* you use the colors depends on which colors you selected. If your favorite colors are neutral colors or colors that flatter your skin tone, you are in luck. You can make these the core colors in your wardrobe and live happily and stylishly ever after. But, if your favorite colors are not flattering on you, you may want to use them in small doses. We will talk more about flattering colors shortly. For now, just make a mental note to reserve favored colors that are not flattering for clothing accents or for handbags, shoes, and other accessories.

Neutral Colors

Neutral colors go with everything. Think of them as the canvas for your wardrobe. You can pair neutral colors with other neutral colors for a timeless look. You can also pair neutral colors with more vibrant colors for a modern twist.

More neutrals means more versatility, because you will be able to mix and match your clothing to create more outfits. You will also be ready for any occasion. Neutral colors are always appropriate…weddings, funerals, parties, the office…they are always safe to wear. But do not confuse safe with boring. Black leather pants are not boring.

Black is the most neutral and versatile color. (Technically, black is the absence of color, but this is not a technical manual.) Black goes with almost everything. It has a slimming effect. It looks classy. It can be dressed up or down. It does not show stains. It is not noticeable if you wear it a lot. You could wear black pants every day for a week and people would not notice, as long as you changed your tops. Try that with bright purple pants.

Additionally, black is flattering on most people. Some people feel it looks too harsh close to their faces. If that is the case for you, you can reserve solid black for pants, skirts, shoes, and other accessories. For tops, dresses, scarves, and other clothing worn near your face, you can wear other colors or wear black as part of a pattern.

Common neutral colors for clothing:

- Black
- Brown
- Cream
- Gray
- Khaki
- Navy
- Olive
- White

This list gives you a good starting point, but colors similar to these are also neutrals. For example, ivory and bone are similar to white and cream. Beige and tan are similar to khaki and brown, etc.

In addition, you can think of the color of blue jeans as a neutral. Whether denim has a light, medium, or dark wash, it goes with practically everything.

The key to determining if a color is neutral is if it looks good with most other colors. So clearly, white is a neutral, but lime green is not.

CHECKLIST ACTION: Choose your favorite neutral colors.

Flattering Colors

We previously discussed color preferences, which are colors that make you *feel* good. Now, let's talk about flattering colors, which are colors that make you *look* good.

To choose flattering colors, consider the impact of...

- Light colors vs. dark colors
- Bright colors vs. muted colors
- Your skin tone

It may be an optical illusion, but dark colors make you look thinner than lighter colors. We already talked about black, but the same principle holds true for charcoal gray, navy blue, chocolate brown, and other dark colors. So if there is an area of your body you would like to appear slimmer, consider clothing in a darker shade for that area.

TIP: Belly bulges and back fat are more noticeable with white and other light-colored clothing. If this is an issue for you, consider wearing lined tops or wearing a camisole underneath unlined tops.

Another consideration is bright vs. muted colors. Our eyes are automatically drawn to bold, vivid colors. So if you want to emphasize your favorite features, wear bright colors in that area. For instance, to show off a small waist, consider a royal blue or neon pink belt. Conversely, if you want to divert attention away from your least favorite features, go with muted colors in that area. This does not mean you have to rule out a color you like. Just choose a muted shade, rather than a bright shade. For instance, if you like red but want to de-emphasize arm flab, wear a brick red top rather than a tomato red top.

The final consideration when it comes to flattering colors is to take your skin tone into account. Skin tones are categorized as cool, warm, or neutral. Women with cool skin tones have pink, red, or blue undertones. Women with warm skin tones have yellow, peach, or gold undertones. Women with neutral skin tones have a mixture of both cool and warm undertones. Different colors look better with different skin tones.

Here are some quick tests to determine your skin tone:

Test 1: Do you look better in white or off-white?
If white, you have a cool skin tone.
If off-white, you have a warm skin tone.
If you look the same in both, you have a neutral skin tone.

Test 2: Do you look better in silver jewelry or gold jewelry?

If silver, you have a cool skin tone.

If gold, you have a warm skin tone.

If you look the same in both, you have a neutral skin tone.

Test 3: Do the veins on the inside of your wrist look blue or green?

If blue, you have a cool skin tone.

If green, you have a warm skin tone.

If somewhere in between, you have a neutral skin tone.

Test 4: Do you burn easily in the sun?

If you burn first and then tan, you have a cool skin tone.

If you tan without burning, you have a warm skin tone.

If you turn pinkish-brown before tanning, you have a neutral skin tone.

Test 5: What is your natural hair color and eye color?

If sandy blond, brown, auburn, or black hair & blue or green eyes, you are cool.

If golden blond, red, or brownish-black hair & brown or hazel eyes, you are warm.

If you are a mixture of the two, you are neutral.

You should now have a good idea of your skin tone. It will help you choose colors that flatter you. After I took the tests, it became clear that I was a cool skin tone. Now I know why whites look good on me, but off-whites make me look washed out and tired.

If you have a cool skin tone, consider clothing that is blue, green, pink, purple, silver, and blue-ish red. In general, colors of the sea and sky look good on cool skin tones. Black and white are especially good neutral colors for cool skin tones.

If you have a warm skin tone, consider clothing that is yellow, orange, gold, yellowish green, and orangey red. In general, earth tones tend to look good on warm skin tones. Gray, brown, and cream are especially good neutral colors for warm skin tones.

If you have a neutral skin tone, you can wear any of the above colors, so pick your favorites.

While the above guidelines are helpful, confirm whether they hold true for you by testing the colors on yourself. You may already naturally gravitate to clothing in colors that flatter you. Take different colored clothing from your closets and hold them up to your face in front of the mirror. Do the same thing when you are considering buying something new. If the color does not flatter you, you may want to pass on the item.

CHECKLIST ACTION: What color is your skin tone? Of the colors that flatter you, list the ones that you especially like. If you like how you look in specific shades of a color – such as navy blue, sky blue, or cobalt blue – list them as well.

Patterns

For maximum versatility, your core wardrobe should consist primarily of solid colors. This allows you to maximize the number of outfits you can create. However, patterns are interesting and fun, so there is definitely a place for them in your wardrobe.

Choosing patterns for your wardrobe is a matter of personal preference, but there are a few things to keep in mind.

First, the smaller the design, the more versatile the article of clothing will be. For instance, picture a jacket with a small, black-and-white houndstooth pattern. It could almost pass as a neutral and will go with many other garments in your wardrobe.

Second, the larger the design, the louder the fabric will appear. Think of the difference between a large floral print versus a small one, large polka dots versus small ones, and large stripes versus small ones. Small prints are generally more stylish, while larger ones can be reminiscent of tablecloths, curtains, and ugly Christmas sweaters.

Third, patterns often look best in small doses. Consider using them mostly on tops, shoes, belts, handbags, or jackets. If a pattern appears on pants, suits, or full-length coats, the clothing can sometimes look too busy.

Fourth, quality construction is a bigger issue when clothing has patterns. With cheaply made clothing, the direction of the print may be off or the design may not line up at the seams. It is particularly noticeable if the stripes on a garment do not line up at the seams.

Fifth, mixing patterns with solids is usually a better look than wearing the same pattern all over. For instance, pairing stripes with solids looks great, but wearing stripes head-to-toe can make you look like you are wearing a prison uniform. Wearing camouflage head-to-toe can make you look like a hunter… and wearing animal prints head-to-toe can make you look like the hunted.

Sixth, if you are very brave, you can sometimes mix different patterns in the same outfit to stylish effect. It is tricky, but the way you can pull it off is to have some continuity between the patterns, such as color. For example, you could wear a floral blouse with small black-

and-white flowers with a pair of pinstriped pants with thin black-and-white stripes.

There are many patterns you could incorporate into your wardrobe. However, just as there are classic styles, there are classic patterns. Following are some classics:

- Animal prints
- Argyle
- Camouflage
- Checks
- Chevron
- Fleur-de-lis
- Floral
- Geometric
- Herringbone
- Houndstooth
- Ikat
- Moroccan
- Paisley
- Plaid
- Polka dot
- Stripes

TIP: If you are not familiar with a particular pattern, search for it on Google Images to help you visualize it.

To personalize your wardrobe, you can also add other patterns that appeal to you. For instance, if you like modern art, an abstract print might be the perfect pattern for a top.

CHECKLIST ACTION: List your favorite patterns.

Styles

When I talk about styles in this section, I am referring to an overall "look" that appeals to you. Sometimes other people influence the way we dress. We may dress to please our husband, boyfriend, or significant other. We may dress to impress the boss. We may dress to fit in with our friends. We may dress to emulate a celebrity we admire.

However, Sara Donaldson, the fashion blogger behind the popular Australian blog, *Harper & Harley*, reminds us that personal style "is about trial and error, but a great way to work this out is to tap into how a color or style makes you feel. Remember to never dress for others, only yourself."

The most authentic way to dress is the one that naturally appeals to you. You may want to tweak or tone down your look for work or personal reasons, but you can still find ways to express your personal style.

For instance, if you work in a conservative office, you may not want to go full-on Goth, but if that is your style, you can certainly wear a lot of black...and maybe tiny little skull earrings.

Following are some common styles. See if any of the descriptions sound like your personal style.

- **Bohemian.** Artsy. Free-spirited. Gypsy. Hippie. Laid-back. Comfortable. Favors peasant blouses, fringe, beads, and long, flowing skirts.

- **Chic.** Elegant. Fashionable. Sophisticated. Socialite. Haute couture. Favors modern cuffs, silky blouses, cashmere sweaters.

- **Classic.** Timeless. Quality. Effortless. Elegance. Polished. Favors peacoats, white button-down blouses, ballet flats, and trench coats.

- **Cool.** Punk. Rocker. Edgy. Anti-materialistic. Anti-establishment. Favors spandex, leopard prints, skinny ripped jeans, tight clothes, and leather jackets.

- **Glamorous.** Dramatic. Attention-grabbing. Sparkling. Bold. Favors diamonds, silk, stilettos, sequin dresses.

- **Minimalist**. Simplicity. Clean lines. Essentials. Unadorned. Modern. Refined. Favors black, tailored jackets, a man's watch.

- **Preppy**. Ivy League. Favors polo shirts, khaki pants, Bermuda shorts, tennis skirts, Lilly Pulitzer dresses, and boat shoes.

- **Romantic.** Feminine. Girly. Ladylike. Dreamy. Idealistic. Favors the color pink, flowery dresses, lacy tops, and ruffles.

- **Sexy.** Flirtatious. Siren. Bare skin. Cleavage. Attention-seeking. Favors tight clothing, stiletto heels, and short skirts, dresses, and shorts.

- **Tomboy**. Simple. Prefers blue to pink. Favors baggy clothes, distressed jeans, graphic tees, and clothing from the boy's department.

- **Western**. Cowgirl. Ranch. Rodeo. Favors denim shirts and jeans, fringe jackets, leather belts with big buckles, turquoise jewelry, cowboy hats, and cowboy boots.

TIP: If one or more of the above styles appeals to you, you can go online to Pinterest, type in the style, and see additional outfit ideas.

Styles tend to reflect how we see ourselves or strive to be. As a result, styles are helpful in building your perfect wardrobe. They do not have to be literal. For instance, you may not live on a ranch or *literally* want to be a cowgirl, but you may like what the western style represents to you. Maybe it symbolizes freedom, or a simpler time, or working with your hands, or the connection to the land. If that is the case, you may want to incorporate certain western elements into your wardrobe. One word of caution: Unless you are a cowgirl, you may not want to wear head-to-toe western wear. Like patterns, a little bit of a style "look" goes a long way.

> CHECKLIST ACTION: Choose one or more styles that appeal to you. You can select styles from the list or come up with your own style description.

In addition...or even instead of...a style, you may have certain themes you like. Unlike styles, a theme may have nothing to do with how you see yourself. You just like how it looks. You could be a pacifist at heart, but still like military clothing because of the way it looks. In the case of a theme, the appeal may be strictly visual or emotional as well.

Here are some common themes. See if any of the themes appeal to you.

- **Ballerinas.** Graceful and elegant. Favors pink and black, ballet flats, flouncy skirts, black velvet ribbons, tulle, voile, and satin fabrics.

- **Beach Chic.** St. Tropez, Capri, the French Riviera. Favors white, linen and cotton, straw bags, scarves, tunics, large sunglasses, and gladiator sandals.

- **Equestrian.** Horseback riding. House in the country. Favors riding boots, breeches, riding jackets, and equestrian motifs on handbags and jewelry.

- **Ethnic or Tribal Prints.** May include Mexican ikat prints, Navajo ganado prints, Pacific Islands tapa prints, Asian batik prints, Moroccan tunics, tribal jewelry, or other looks common to a specific culture.

- **Global Fashion Capitals.** Paris, Milan, London, and New York are the fashion capitals of the world. Paris is known as the birthplace of haute couture, and many women admire the French chic look. Milan is known for beautiful and seductive looks. London is known for edgy, street styles. New York is known for casual, sporty looks.

- **Menswear.** Any look borrowed from men. Favors menswear trousers, men's button-down shirts, tweed jackets, ties, vests, and loafers.

- **Military.** Inspired by any branch of the military. Favors camouflage, utility jackets, khaki pants, navy blazer with gold buttons, and aviator sunglasses.

- **Motorcycles.** Biker look. Favors black, leather biker jackets, Harley Davidson clothing, and moto leather boots.

- **Nautical.** Inspired by the sea. Favors red, white, and navy blue stripes, the anchor motif, boat shoes, espadrilles, and ropes on belts, totes, and jewelry.

- **Vintage.** A look borrowed from any former era: the 20's flappers, the 40's Hollywood glamour, the 50's rock & roll, the swinging 60's, the 70's disco, etc.

TIP: If one or more of the above themes appeals to you, you can go online to Pinterest, type in the theme, and see additional outfit ideas.

CHECKLIST ACTION: Choose one or more themes that appeal to you. You can select themes from the list or come up with your own themes.

Step 4

Know What Fits and Flatters Your Body

T he fourth step in the *Style & Clothing System* is to choose clothes that fit well and flatter your body type. When it comes to looking good in your clothes, the number one factor is fit. The most beautiful clothes in the world will not look good on you if they fit poorly. Closely related to proper fit is choosing the types of clothing most flattering to your body. What flatters you will depend on your shape, size, and other physical features.

Once you know how clothes should fit and what styles flatter you, shopping for clothes will be easier. You can buy clothes that work for you, or you can make them work for you with simple alterations.

One of the reasons it is so hard to find clothes that fit properly is that we buy ready-to-wear clothing. There was a time when many people made their own clothes, but now most of us buy everything off the rack. That would be fine if we were all the same shape, but we are not. Fashion designers and clothing manufacturers generally use one fit model per size, and that model often has an hourglass shape. So even if you are the same size as the model, the clothing may not fit you right if she has an hourglass shape and you have more of a pear, apple, or straight shape.

To add to the difficulty of finding clothes that fit, different brands size their clothing differently. A size 8 in one brand may be a size 6 or 10 in another. My advice is to ignore the size and go by fit, which we will discuss shortly.

Another issue that affects how our clothing fits is that our weight and shape change over time. Having children, getting older, becoming less active, and eating more, can all change the shape and size of our bodies. Women react to these changes in different ways. Some change their clothing to fit their changing bodies. Some continue wearing the same clothing even if it is too tight. Some begin wearing shapeless clothing in an attempt to hide their bodies.

Debbie Mikulla, owner of Closet Control and a consultant for the Etcetera clothing line, tells her clients, "You have to dress the body you have now." That is great advice. By wearing clothes that fit your current body, you will look and feel better. If you instead try to squeeze into clothes that do not fit or wear tent-like clothing, you will look and feel worse. If you lose weight through dieting or change your shape through exercise, you can always have your clothes taken in by a tailor...but why not look your best in the meantime by wearing clothes that fit you *now?*

Proper Fit

You can tell if clothing fits you properly by looking in a full-length mirror. The most flattering fit is neither too tight, nor too loose. The best look for most women is clothing that is slightly fitted, meaning it skims the body without hugging it. This fit flatters your silhouette, and adds instant style and polish. If you can see any unsightly bulges through your clothes in front or back, your clothes are too tight. If you cannot even see your figure underneath your clothes, they are too loose. If any part of the clothing gapes, bunches up, twists around, pulls, tugs, rides up, or droops down, it does not fit properly.

Following are some general guidelines on how your clothes should fit:

- **Bras.** The band should be at the same level all the way around. It should not pull up in the back. The center piece between the cups should lie flat against your skin. The straps should not dig into your skin or fall off your shoulder. The cups should be smooth with no gaping, and your breasts should not spill out the sides. A bra fit specialist at a boutique or department store can measure you to ensure you get the right fit. A proper-fitting bra makes a big difference in how your breasts look under your clothes, so it is worth getting this one right.

- **Panties.** Like bras, the panties you wear can make a huge difference in how your clothes look. Visible panty lines are not attractive. Some women wear a thong to avoid VPL. While I wear them occasionally (especially with white pants), I find lace boyshorts and hipsters work just as well and are far more comfortable. I especially like the ones from Hanky Panky and Victoria's Secret. It is important that you find a size and style that fits you well, or your underwear will dig into your skin or ride up. It is hard to look stylish when you are pulling your panties out of your crack or crotch!

TIP: If you want to simplify your intimates, buy all your bras and panties in either black or nude. Your nude color should be based on your skin tone, regardless of what color is listed on the tag. I like white, too, but it sometimes shows under white clothing. If you stick to black and nude, you will be good to go regardless of what clothes you are wearing. Keep it simple.

- **Tops.** Pay attention to where the shoulder seam connects the sleeve to the body of your top. If the seam is too close to your neck, the top will look too small. If the seam extends past your shoulder, the top will look too big. In addition, check to make sure the fabric that covers your bust fits smoothly and does not pull too tight or hang too loose. The top should be long enough that your skin is not exposed when you bend over or sit down. If you have to keep pulling your shirt down or tucking it back in, it is too short. If you are wearing a blouse, you should be able to button the blouse with no pulling across your chest and no gaping between buttons.

- **Jeans.** Finding jeans that fit you in the waist, hips, thighs, butt, and legs is no easy feat. So if you find a brand you like, stick with it. The waistband of the jeans should sit flush against your skin, with no gap in back. If they balloon out in front, sag in the butt, or cause you to keep pulling up on the waistband, they are too big. If they dig into your skin or cause muffin top or back cleavage, they are too small. Mid-rise jeans work well for many women, but it is all about proportion. If you are short-waisted, you may want low-rise jeans. Otherwise, it may look like your jeans start right under your breasts. If you are long-waisted, you may want high-rise jeans. Otherwise, it may look like you have short legs. As for ultra-low-rise jeans, they really do not look good on anyone...except perhaps supermodels.

- **Pants.** Most casual and dress pants are mid-rise. They should fit comfortably at the waist, without gaping or digging into your skin. If there is pulling, wrinkling, or creasing across the stomach, butt, or thighs when you are standing, the pants are too small. If the pants poof out when you sit down, they are too big. The zipper should stay up, and the fabric around the zipper should not pull. Even if the pants fit you well, it is not uncommon for the pockets to flare out when you sit down. If this happens, you can have a tailor remove the pockets or sew them shut.

- **Skirts.** A skirt that fits properly will not shift around when you walk. It should fit smoothly against your hips. If it clings to your hips and then flares out, it is too tight in the hips. It is better to buy a skirt that fits in the hips even if it is too big in the waist. You can always have the waist taken in by a tailor.

- **Dresses.** The fit in the shoulders is key for dresses. The shoulder seam should be at the edge of your shoulder. Otherwise, the dress will not hang right. If a dress has a fitted waist, make sure the waist of the dress lines up with your waist. If you have trouble finding dresses that fit you in the shoulders, bust, waist, or hips, consider a wrap dress or a shift dress. These styles are more accommodating to different body shapes.

- **Blazers and Jackets.** The shoulder seam for a blazer or jacket should be right at the edge of your shoulder. If it is closer to your neck, it is too small. If it hangs off your shoulder, it is too large. You should be able to hug someone without feeling constricted through the shoulders. Otherwise, the blazer or jacket is too small. Most jackets should look and feel slightly fitted, unless you are wearing a boxy jacket, which is supposed to be looser. If you are large busted, you will be happy to know that an open jacket is acceptable in today's more casual world. Rather than buy a jacket that is too big in the shoulders in order to accommodate your bust, you can just leave your jacket open.

When you go into a clothing store, you can grab a couple different sizes to find your best fit. However, many of us shop online. To avoid getting stuck with ill-fitting clothes, shop mainly with companies that offer free shipping and returns, like Nordstrom and Zappos.

TIP: Keep an updated list of your measurements: bust, waist, hips, inseam, and torso. (If you wear one-piece swimsuits, stores like J. Crew offer long-torso options.) When you shop online, you can compare your measurements to the store's size chart to ensure you order the correct size for that brand.

Alterations

Finding clothing that fits your body perfectly is great. However, if you find a style you like that is "almost" perfect, you may be able to get it altered.

If you do not sew and have no desire to learn, ask a stylish friend or family member to recommend a good tailor. You can also ask for a recommendation from stylists in clothing boutiques or department stores. Some stores offer free alterations for clothing you buy from them.

Bear in mind that some alterations are worth making...and some are not. An alteration is only worthwhile if the cost is reasonable. A simple alteration will obviously cost less than a complicated one. Additionally, it makes more sense to alter a higher quality garment than it does to alter a cheap one. Finally, an alteration should only be made if it will not ruin the outline or overall look of the garment.

Alterations that are worth making:
- Taking a shirt in at the seams
- Slimming sleeves that are too wide
- Hemming jeans, pants, skirts, tops, and dresses
- Adding darts to a skirt that is too big at the waist
- Narrowing the inseams of pants that are too loose

Alterations that are usually NOT worth making:

- Poor quality clothing
- Anything with a lining
- Anything that is too small
- Clothing made of leather, suede, or lace
- Clothes with pleats, beads, sequins, or other embellishments

TIP: If you buy an article of clothing and are not sure it can be altered, take it to an alterations place before you remove the tags. If the tailor says it cannot be altered, you can still return it for a refund.

Styles that Flatter Your Body Type

Most women can be loosely categorized as having one of four body shapes, commonly called:

- **Hourglass.** Shoulders and hips are the same width and the waist is smaller.
- **Straight (Rectangle).** Shoulders, hips, and waist are the same width.
- **Pear (Triangle).** Hips are wider than shoulders and waist.
- **Apple (Inverted Triangle).** Shoulders are wider than hips and waist.

Of course, these four categories do not even begin to capture all our different body shapes, but they are useful for discussion purposes. The idea is to look at your silhouette and find clothing styles that flatter your figure. The most attractive styles are those that create the appearance of balance and proportion.

For hourglass body types, look for clothing that emphasizes your curves and draws attention to your waist. Flattering styles include fitted v-neck tops or sweaters, skinny or straight-leg jeans and pants, pencil skirts, wrap or belted dresses, and single-breasted jackets that come to the hip or hit just below your butt.

For straight body types, look for clothing that shows off your athletic build while adding curves, ruching, or other details. Flattering styles include cap-sleeve or scoopneck tops, straight-leg or skinny jeans, pleated pants, tiered or pleated skirts, A-line or shift dresses, and peplum jackets.

For pear body types, look for clothing that plays up your feminine shape, while balancing out your hips by adding width to your shoulders and the lowest part of your body. Flattering styles include boatneck tops and cardigan sweaters, bootcut or flared jeans, wide-leg pants, A-line skirts and dresses, and structured jackets with light padding or shoulder details.

For apple body types, look for clothing that softens your strong shoulders and accentuates your lower body. Flattering styles include v-neck tops and sweaters, feminine blouses, bootcut and high-rise jeans, wide-leg pants, full skirts and dresses, and longer, unstructured jackets.

The objective of the above suggestions is to achieve symmetry and balance. But to work for you, your clothes also have to fit your style. For instance, if you have a straight body type but prefer a menswear or military theme over a romantic style, you may not want pleated skirts or peplum jackets. No problem; just add different details. So instead of a peplum jacket, get a military style jacket with epaulets on the shoulders. Whatever works for you.

> CHECKLIST ACTION: Note your body type and styles of clothing that flatter your shape and fit your style.

If there is anything about your body that you do not like, you are not alone. I asked Marti Gordon, a personal stylist for *The Fifth Avenue Club* at Saks Fifth Avenue, what issues women struggle with when choosing their wardrobe. She said, "Most women are not comfortable with their body...I do not know one woman that is totally happy with their body. I try to help them find their best features and accentuate that feature. It helps when the client is confident wearing what she has on."

None of us are physically perfect, but we can use different clothing styles to emphasize our favorite features or de-emphasize our least favorite features. For instance, if you love your long, graceful neck, you might want to wear turtlenecks to show it off. If you do not care for your upper arms or elbows, you can wear three-quarter sleeves to cover them.

For some of us, getting older creates changes in our skin that we do not love. We can address these issues through clothing choices. For example, if you have sun damage on your chest, you may prefer crewneck tops instead of deep v-neck tops. If you have spider veins on your legs, you may choose to wear ankle-length capris rather than shorts.

Jessica Landez, the owner of BluePeppermint Boutique, said, "We hear people say they are 'too old' to wear this or wear that BUT we just don't agree! You might want to wear a cami or a bralette or a pair of spanx, but most styles are appropriate for most ages when tailored to flatter your body." There is no reason why you cannot continue to wear your favorite styles as you get older. You may just want to modify them.

Just remember to make choices based on *your* preferences, not what other people think or say.

Regardless of your shape, weight, height, or age, you can find clothing to help you look and feel your best.

True style comes from within, not just from without. I am reminded of a great line in a song by Jack Johnson called *Posters*. It says, "Well, I'm an energetic, hypothetic, version of another person. Check out my outsides, there ain't nothing in here." Of course, I see no reason why we cannot be both...beautiful on the inside *and* out.

Step 5

Decide What Quality and Quantity of Clothing You Want

- - - - - - - - - - - - - - - -

The fifth step in the *Style & Clothing System* is to determine what quality and quantity of clothing makes sense for you. This is partly a financial issue and partly a personal issue.

If you have a limited budget for clothing, you will

need to make trade-offs between quality and quantity. You may be like the chic French woman who chooses quality over quantity. She may have a much smaller wardrobe than the typical American woman, but her garments are more versatile and of a higher quality. You can decide whether you want to have more clothes of a lower quality, fewer clothes of a higher quality, or something in between.

From a personal standpoint, it is important to think about what is important to you. Are you trying to simplify your life? Then you may want fewer clothes, even if money is no object. Do you like the finer things in life? Then you may want higher quality clothes, even if you have to save up for them. Is variety the spice of life for you? Then you may want a higher quantity of clothes, and quality may be secondary. Are you concerned about the ethical treatment of factory workers? Then you may want to pay a little more for clothes made in factories where workers are fairly treated. Are you concerned about the environment? Then you may want fewer clothes that you can wear longer to avoid waste.

The important thing is to give some thought to the quality and quantity of clothing that makes sense based on what you value most.

Quality

Higher quality clothing looks and feels better than cheaply made clothing. It would be convenient if price alone were an indicator of quality, but that is not always the case. Higher quality clothing does tend to cost more than cheaper clothing. However, the higher cost is not entirely due to higher quality materials and labor. Some brands charge substantially more for their clothing to cover their marketing and advertising costs and their profit margins. High-end designer brands can charge excessive prices, because customers are willing to pay for the designer name.

To recognize true quality regardless of price, look at the fabric and construction of the garment. In addition, if you are going to invest in quality, you will want to know how to care for your higher quality garments. So let's move into the discussion of the three primary factors that affect quality: fabric, construction, and care.

Fabric

Better quality fabrics look better and last longer than cheaper fabrics. They also hold their shape, are breathable, and move with you. You can sometimes tell a cheap, synthetic fabric just by looking at it – it may appear too stiff, too thin, or too shiny. You can also tell a synthetic fabric by wearing it. Unlike natural fabrics, synthetics do not allow your skin to breathe. As a result, synthetics may make you feel hot and sweaty when worn in warmer temperatures.

Natural fabrics commonly used in higher quality clothing include:

- **Cashmere.** A soft fabric that adds warmth without bulk. This lightweight fabric is mainly used for sweaters. It can be worn on its own, but it is also thin enough to be layered. Scarves can also be made of cashmere. Better quality cashmeres are two-ply and up. The highest quality cashmere comes from Italy or Scotland.

- **Cotton.** A breathable fabric widely used for T-shirts, tops, blouses, blue jeans, other denim garments, pants, skirts, dresses, light-weight jackets, etc. Especially good for warmer weather. Pima is the highest quality cotton.

- **Silk.** An elegant fabric that drapes well and is often used for blouses, evening gowns, robes, lingerie, dressy suits, and the lining in clothing. The highest quality silks have a heavier weight than other silks.

- **Wool.** A durable fabric that comes in a variety of weights. The lighter weights, like gabardine, are used for all-seasons suiting. The medium weights are used for skirts, pants, and suits. The heaviest weights are used for jackets and winter coats.

- **Leather.** While leather is not technically a fabric, I am including it here because it is commonly used to make high-quality jackets, coats, pants, shoes, and handbags. Examples of high-quality leathers are lambskin for pants, jackets and coats; calfskin and alligator skin for shoes; and full grain cowhide leather for handbags.

There are other natural fabrics that you may want to consider, but none are as versatile as the ones above. For instance, linen is a natural fabric that is good for keeping you cool in the summer. However, it wrinkles easily so it is not ideal if you are looking for low-maintenance clothing. Hemp is another natural fabric, but it is not as soft as cotton.

Although synthetic fabrics are lower in quality than natural fabrics, you may not want to rule them out completely. Synthetics can help clothing resist wrinkles and stains. In addition, some synthetics give jeans and other clothing a little stretch. I recommend no more than 1 to 3 percent of elasticity, or your jeans can bag at the knees. The most common synthetic fabrics used in clothing are acetate, acrylic, nylon, polyester, rayon, and spandex.

TIP: Pay attention to the labels on your clothing. If you have clothes that look and feel especially nice, note whether they include natural fabrics, synthetic fabrics, or a blend of both. Do the same with clothing that looks or feels cheap to you. Just like reading labels on food, you will come to know which fabrics you like and which you dislike by reading the labels on your clothes.

CHECKLIST ACTION: Make a list of the fabrics you like, and any you would prefer to avoid.

Construction

The construction of an article of clothing has a major impact on quality. The construction determines how a garment looks and feels. It also affects how long it lasts before buttons fall off, zippers get stuck, and the fabric comes apart at the seams.

You can spot high quality construction by checking:

- **Buttons.** They should be firmly attached, not hanging on by a thread. Better quality clothing often comes with extra buttons, particularly for shirts and sweaters.

- **Zippers.** They should lie flat and zip smoothly up and down. If the zipper snags on the fabric, it is not well constructed. If the zipper is supposed to be hidden, it should be completely hidden. For instance, the flap over the zipper of your jeans should completely conceal your zipper. If you can see part of the fabric around the zipper, the clothing is not well made.

- **Seams.** They should be straight. Seams on cheaper garments often wind around to the front. You should be able to fold a pair of pants lengthwise, and the seams for the right and left leg should line up exactly. For a top, the side seams and sleeve seams should also line up on the right and left side. Seams should lie flat and have no loose threads. Repeating patterns, like stripes, should evenly line up at the seams.

- **Hems.** They should be smooth with no puckering. If there is decorative or contrast stitching (where the thread is a different color than the fabric), the stitching should be even all the way around. Otherwise, the stitching should not be visible from the outside of the garment. Higher quality garments have more stitches per inch.

- **Pockets**. The inside of the pockets should not be visible from the outside of the garment. With lower-quality pants, you can sometimes see the outline of the pocket through the pants. Additionally, if the pockets are a different color on the inside than the outside, you should not be able to see the inside color. For instance, since denim is so bulky, the inside pockets of jeans are normally a lighter color and fabric. You should not be able to see that fabric peeking out of your pockets.

- **Lining.** The lining should not be visible from the outside. It should neither hang down below the garment, nor show through it. If it bunches up or is stiff, that is an indicator of poor quality. A quality lining will result in a garment that hangs correctly.

- **Embellishments.** If the garment has beads, sequins, or other types of embellishments, they should be securely attached. Additionally, they should not pull or stretch the fabric around them.

In addition to the specific items above, you can tell if a garment is well constructed by the overall look of it. Quality garments just look better. They seamlessly transition from thick to thin. For instance, you should not see bulging where there are pockets or at the seams.

Poor quality is much more obvious if you turn a garment inside out. You will be able to see the crooked stitching, puckering, and loose threads more easily. Even if you cannot see the quality defects from the outside, they will affect how the garment looks on you. Poor construction is the reason a top may not hang right or pants may not look right, even if you cannot put your finger on the reason.

Poor quality may not be as noticeable the first time

you wear the garment. However, over time the defects will become obvious as hems unravel and buttons fall off.

Care

Taking good care of your clothing extends the life of all garments, but it is especially important for your higher quality clothing. Some elements of good care take no extra time, so they are no-brainers. Other aspects of good care are more time-consuming, so only you can decide if you are willing to do them.

Tips for caring for clothing:

- **Read the care label.** At the risk of sounding obvious, the label on your clothes will provide information on how to properly care for them. The Federal Trade Commission requires care labels on all clothing.

- **Turn clothing inside out when washing.** This will cause less fading and is especially important for clothing with patterns, graphics, or embellishments. It is also helpful for jeans and dark clothing.

- **Avoid fabric softeners.** They can cause garments to age more quickly. Also, activewear clothing often has wicking technology to keep you cooler when working out. If you use fabric softeners, they leave a coating on clothing that interferes with the wicking technology.

- **Dry-clean sparingly.** The chemicals used by traditional dry cleaners can weaken the fabric and may be toxic. If a garment says "dry-clean only" but you are worried about toxicity, you may want to try a green dry cleaning service. You can also go longer between dry cleaning visits if you rotate your clothing and use an inexpensive handheld steamer at home.

- **Use cold water and air dry when possible.** Cold water will prevent clothes from fading. Air drying will prevent clothes from shrinking. Intimate apparel, cashmere, and silk can all be hand-washed in cold water and air dried, as long as the label says "dry-clean" as opposed to "dry-clean only." After washing, reshape your garments and lay them flat to dry.

- **Know when to hang and when to fold.** Many experts recommended folding cashmere and knit clothing, because hanging can stretch them out and leave shoulder bumps. You may want to fold turtlenecks as well, because the long necks make them difficult to hang. Besides intimates, workout clothes, and smaller clothing items like swimsuits, shorts, and tanks, I prefer to hang everything else. Hanging avoids wrinkles caused by folding and allows you to see what you have to wear. Use padded hangers for delicate fabrics like silk, satin, chiffon, velvet, or taffeta. Use curved suit hangers for preserving the shape of jackets and blazers. Use hangers with clips for skirts. Use wooden hangers or hangers with clamps for pants and jeans. For most other clothing, like tops, blouses, or dress-es, you can use basic shirt or dress hangers.

- **Do not overcrowd your closets and drawers.** Clothes need to breathe to air out any odors. Also, overcrowding causes clothes to wrinkle. Leave about an inch between hangers. Once you implement your clothing system, you will need fewer clothes so overcrowding should not be a problem.

Taking good care of your clothes does take a lit-tle more work. If you are willing to do the extra work, your clothes will thank you by looking better and last-ing longer.

Quantity

The quantity of clothing you need depends upon many factors, such as your preferences, budget, closet space, and lifestyle. In this section, I am going to talk about ways to streamline your wardrobe. Some of these strategies will sound familiar; others are new. You can tailor the advice to suit your needs.

You can reduce the quantity of clothing you need by...

- **Choosing higher quality clothing.** As we pre-viously discussed, purchasing higher quality clothes and taking good care of them will cause them to last longer. Since you will not need to replace them as frequently, you will need fewer clothes overall.

- **Focusing on classics rather than trends.** It is fun to buy some trendy clothes as long as they fit your style and look good on you. In fact, Marti Gordon, a personal stylist for *The Fifth Avenue Club* at Saks Fifth Avenue, recommends that you "purchase a few new 'trends' for the season (spring and fall) and incorporate them into your existing wardrobe." However, if trendy clothes are a big part of your wardrobe, you will need to replace them constantly. Since classics are timeless, making them the foundation of your wardrobe results in needing fewer clothes.

- **Picking colors, patterns, and styles that work well together.** If you primarily choose neutral colors for your base wardrobe – supplemented with complementary colors, patterns, and styles – you will be able to mix and match to create more outfits with fewer clothes.

- **Changing your lifestyle.** Where and how you live affects the quantity of clothing you need. Of course, it would not make sense to change your lifestyle just to reduce your clothing needs. But if you were thinking of making a change anyway, like simplifying your life or moving to a warmer climate, you may also reduce the number of clothes you need in the process. When I resigned my position as vice president of financial planning for an insurance company, I no longer needed all my corporate clothes. Without the steady paycheck, I also became more reluctant to waste money on clothes I did not really want or need. Simplifying is helping me build a better wardrobe with fewer clothes.

- **Wearing season-transitioning wardrobe pieces.** Rather than buying clothing for each season and weather condition, you can look for clothing that works for multiple seasons and weather. Instead of buying separate coats for spring and fall, you can buy a trench coat with a removable liner. If winters are relatively mild where you live, you may even be able to wear the coat in the winter. Rather than buying rain or snow boots, you can waterproof your regular ankle boots or knee-high boots or buy weather-proof brands.

- **Layering your clothes.** Layering is a great alternative to buying separate clothes for different temperatures, occasions, and activities. Rather than buying heavier clothing that can only be worn when it is cold outside, you can layer your clothes and wear them year-around. Layering also works when it is warm outside, but air conditioning makes it chilly inside. In addition, layering can help you dress an outfit up or down. If you throw a denim jacket over a white blouse, you dress it down. If you instead throw a tuxedo jacket over the blouse, you dress it up. Finally, layering allows you to pack fewer clothes when you travel. You can change your look for different activities just by switching out certain pieces. I will talk more about how to effectively layer in Step 8, when we talk about outfits. For now, just note that it is another way to lower the quantity of clothing you need.

- **Buying more tops than bottoms.** You can reduce the number of clothes you need by adopting a 2-to-1, 3-to-1, or even a 4-to-1 ratio of tops to bottoms. People notice tops more than pants or skirts. Unless you are wearing skintight jeans, a micro-miniskirt, or a bodycon dress, people are usually looking up at your face. A higher ratio of tops to bottoms also dovetails nicely with the strategy of choosing solid, neutral colors for pants, skirts, and shorts. If you have chosen black as one of your neutral colors, how many pairs of black pants do you really need? As long as you pair them with different tops, you can create many different outfits with fewer bottoms.

- **Matching clothes to shoe styles and heights.** We will talk more about shoes in the next step of the *Style & Clothing System*. The point here is that you can reduce the quantity of clothes you need if you skillfully pair them with your shoes. A common issue is buying a pair of shoes you like, but then realizing they do not look right with your clothes. Then you need to buy more clothes to work with that style of shoe. The same thing can happen when the heel heights of your shoes do not work with your clothes. You buy a great pair of shoes, but the pants you were going to wear with them are too long or too short.

When I originally did my closet audit, I realized I had 43 pairs of shoes with 10 different heel heights: flat, .5 inches, 1 inch, 1.5 inches, 2 inches, 2.5 inches, 3 inches, 3.5 inches, 4 inches, and 4.5 inches. That required more pants of varying lengths to work with all my different heel heights. I noticed the most common heel heights in my closet were flats and 3-inch heels. Now when I shop for shoes, I take a cloth measuring tape with me (yes, really) and mainly buy flats or shoes with 3-inch heels. This allows me to buy, or alter, my jeans and pants to fit just two heel heights, which reduces the quantity of clothing I need.

> CHECKLIST ACTION: Note all of the quantity-reducing strategies that appeal to you.

Choosing the quality and quantity of clothing you desire is a personal decision. There is no right or wrong answer. The most important part is to be mindful about your clothing choices. Stop to think about what you really want and need. The result will be a wardrobe that is more versatile, more stylish, and more personalized for you.

Step 6

Pick Your Shoes, Handbags, Jewelry, and Other Accessories

The sixth step in the *Style & Clothing System* is to choose the shoes, handbags, jewelry, and other accessories that will complete your look. Clothing may be the opening act, but our accessories often steal the show. As we have been discussing, the secret to a perfect wardrobe is versatility, style, and personalization. Your accessories allow you to tick off all three boxes.

Accessories provide versatility by allowing you to create different looks with the same clothes. Picture a simple white T-shirt and dark jeans. Add a peace sign necklace, flip-flops, and a leather fringe bag, and you have one look. Add a black pearl necklace, black stilettos, and a quilted Chanel bag with a chain strap, and you have a completely different look. By simply changing your accessories, you can change your look.

Your accessories provide style through their ability to transform an otherwise plain or boring outfit. A plain black dress with plain black pumps is bland. Add a gold link necklace and arm bangles, and switch out the black pumps for a pair in snakeskin, and you have a more stylish outfit.

Accessories also provide you with a perfect opportunity to personalize your look. You and a thousand other people may buy the exact same white blouse. But if you personalize yours by cinching it at the waist with a turquoise belt you picked up on your travels, you will have made it your own.

An additional benefit of accessories is that they continue to fit you even as you get older or your weight fluctuates. Your handbag and jewelry do not care if you put on five pounds. They will still look good on you.

With age, your shoe size might gradually change but usually no more than a half-size every 10-plus years. That is a long time to wear a pair of shoes!

Neutral colors for accessories are similar, but not identical, to neutral colors for clothing.

Neutral colors for shoes, handbags, and jewelry:
- Black
- Brown
- Gold
- Gray
- Navy
- Nude
- Silver
- Tan
- White

> TIP: Nude shoes can elongate your legs, making you appear taller. Remember to choose a nude color that is close to your skin tone for the best look.

Shoes

When it comes to shoes, it is easy to be seduced by a pretty face. We see a beautiful pair of shoes in a store, in a magazine, or on another woman's feet, and we just have to have them. They are gorgeous, and it is love at first sight. But first impressions are not always right.

Before you think about buying any pair of shoes, make sure you can answer "yes" to the following questions:

1. Do they fit?
2. Are they comfortable?
3. Do they flatter your feet?
4. Do they go with the clothes in your closet?

If the answer to any of the questions is "no," do not buy them. If you do, they will more than likely sit in your closet gathering dust.

For shoes to fit you properly, they should conform to the shape of your feet. No part of your foot...toes, ball, heel...should hang over or off the shoe. If your heel hangs off the back of the shoe, the shoes are too small. If the ball of your feet spills off the sides, your shoes are too narrow. If your toes hang off the front of the shoe when you sit or stand, the shoes are too small. If your toes only hang off when you walk, you may just need pads (like Foot Petals), to keep your feet from sliding forward.

If you can put a finger between your heel and the back of the shoe, the shoes are too big. Also, if your shoes ride up and down on your heel when you walk, they are too big. If you cannot wiggle your toes in closed-toe shoes, the shoes are too small.

TIP: Many people have one foot that is slightly larger than the other one, so be sure the shoes fit your largest foot. Additionally, you may need to go up a half-size for pointy-toe shoes.

If your shoes do not fit, they are likely to be uncomfortable. However, sometimes even shoes that do fit are uncomfortable. For example, I have sensitive feet, so I cannot wear flip-flops or any other shoe with a thong; it leaves a blister between my toes. Additionally, cheap shoes can cause problems. A poorly made strap can rub against your ankle. Prominent seams inside the shoe may rub against your feet. A cheaply made sole may hurt your feet when you walk.

If a shoe is not comfortable, you will not wear it. It does not matter how cute the shoe is, you will rarely wear shoes that hurt your feet. It also does not matter if you got them on sale. If you get a $150 pair of shoes for $50 and they hurt your feet, you did not save $100… you wasted $50.

Also, it is hard to look stylish in uncomfortable shoes. Limping, wincing, complaining, and rubbing your feet detracts from any style the shoes may have otherwise given you.

If the shoes pass the fit and comfort test, check to

see if they flatter your feet. Put them on and look at them in a mirror.

If your feet are larger, you may find shoes with heels are more flattering than flat shoes. You may also find that your feet will look smaller if you wear darker shoes or shoes with accents, like buckles. Finally, you may want to avoid pointy-toe shoes and skimpy sandals.

If your toes are callused or you just do not like how they look, you may want to wear peep-toe or closed-toe shoes. When you wear sandals, look for a pair with more coverage across the toes.

As with clothing, proportion and balance are important. If you have thin legs, chunky shoes can make your feet look huge and pointy flats can make your feet look long. If you are a larger woman, dainty shoes can make you look heavier.

If the veins on your feet bother you, you may not want to wear thin, strappy sandals that expose most of your feet. Instead, wear sandals with more coverage.

If you do not like how a pair of shoes looks on you, pass on them. Hold out for a more flattering pair.

As a final test, ask yourself whether you have anything in your closet to wear with the shoes. If you have a closet full of casual clothes to go with your casual lifestyle, those sparkly evening shoes you are eyeing will not get much use. Heel height is another consideration. If you mainly wear bootcut jeans and pants, those gorgeous ballet flats you are considering are not going to get much wear.

It is easy to make impulse purchases when it comes to shoes. When you see a pair you like, it is tempting to buy them without thinking it through. You view the shoes in isolation, rather than thinking of them in the bigger wardrobe picture. If you instead ask yourself the four questions from the beginning of this shoe section, you will begin to upgrade your shoe selection.

If you cannot resist the impulse to buy, at least keep the receipts. Wear the shoes around the house and try them on with some of your clothes. If they are not going to work out, return them. Then you will get the rush of the purchase, but without buyer's remorse.

Instant gratification feels good, but so does delayed gratification. For example, think about how much fun it is too look forward to a vacation. Rather than buy so-so shoes now, hold out for shoes that you will really love. You will get a lot more enjoyment and wear out of the shoes in the long run.

While there are an endless number of shoe styles, you can narrow down the types to these five:

- Flats
- Sandals
- Boots

- Pumps
- Sneakers

TIP: When choosing among the types and styles of shoes, think about what fits and flatters your body and feet, your lifestyle, your preferences, and the types of clothes you wear. You will find additional information about what types of shoes to wear with different types of clothing in Step 8, where we will talk about putting together outfits.

Flats

Flats are a versatile shoe that you can wear with shorts, skirts, dresses, or pants. They are comfortable and provide a stylish alternative to sneakers. You can wear most flats year around. They are particularly nice to wear in early spring when it is not quite warm enough for sandals, and in early fall when it is not quite cold enough for boots. Flats are also great for travel. You can easily slip them on and off at the airport, and they do not take up much room in your suitcase. Most flats look best with bare feet, though oxfords and loafers are sometimes worn with thin socks or tights.

Common styles of flats are ballet flats, espadrilles, loafers, moccasins, and oxfords.

Ballet flats are a feminine, classic shoe. Espadrilles are a shoe with woven rope, perfect for summer. Loafers are a comfortable, menswear-inspired shoe. Moccasins are an ultra casual, slip-on shoe. Oxfords are a preppy, lace-up shoe.

If you are only buying one pair of flats, you may want to pick a neutral color that works well with most of the clothes you will wear with them. Also consider when you will mainly wear them. If in warmer months, consider lighter colors. If in cooler months, consider darker colors. A metallic color works year around.

Once you have found the style (or styles) of flats you like best, you may want to buy more in different colors or patterns. Flats with thin stripes, animal prints, or bold colors can add a modern feel to more neutral clothing. You can also add visual interest to flats with accents, like a metal-capped toe.

To ensure your flats remain stylish, you may want to avoid extreme shapes. An almond toe works better for flats than a toe that is overly round, overly pointed, or overly square. An almond toe has a slightly rounded, pointed toe. The most classic ballet flats are made by Repetto...they have an almond toe.

> CHECKLIST ACTION: Pick your favorite styles of flats. Add notes, such as preferred colors, patterns, and accents. Also note whether you prefer different flats for different seasons.

Sandals

Sandals are another versatile shoe style. They are great to wear in the summer and also for dressier occasions. More than likely, you will want at least one casual, flat or low-heeled sandal for daytime and one dressier, higher-heeled sandal for evening.

Common styles of sandals are ankle-strap, block heel, flip-flop, gladiator, slide, and wedge.

Ankle-strap sandals are a classic style that can be flat or heeled and either dressy or casual. Block heel sandals have a sturdier heel, making them easier to walk in. Flip-flops are an ultra casual sandal, perfect for the beach or pool. Gladiator sandals may actually lace up around the legs, or just be styled to look like the shoes worn by ancient Roman gladiators. Slide sandals are a backless, slip-on sandal, and are a casual and comfortable shoe. Wedge sandals have a triangular, wedge-shaped heel that is also the sole. The wedge is often covered by rope, just like espadrille flats.

You may want to start with a casual sandal in a flat or small heel for summer. If you wear sandals a lot, it is worth investing in at least one pair of higher-quality leather sandals in a neutral color that will work with most of your summer clothes.

Once you have your go-to, comfortable, classic sandal, you can choose additional sandals that reflect your personal preferences and style. For instance, if you love the nautical theme, you may like espadrille wedge sandals with navy & white stripes. It can be fun to have a bright or patterned pair of sandals to liven up your wardrobe. You can also buy sandals with interesting accents like cutouts, rhinestones, contrast stitching, beads, studs, buckles, braiding, fringe, or other details.

For dressier evening sandals, consider ankle-strap metallic sandals with a higher heel. If you have a warm skin tone, you may like strappy, gold sandals. If you have a cool skin tone, consider silver sandals. Black is another great option for evening sandals.

When choosing heeled sandals, remember to think about heel heights. If you stick with a few heel heights you like, you will be able to wear your sandals with more of your clothes. This is particularly important if you wear pants more often than skirts and dresses.

Finally, if you are going to wear sandals, remember to groom your feet. The most gorgeous sandals in the world will not look stylish if your heels are cracked, your toes are callused, and your toenail polish is chipping!

CHECKLIST ACTION: Pick your favorite styles of sandals. Add notes, such as preferred colors, patterns, and accents. Also, note which style you prefer for daytime and which you prefer for evenings.

Boots

Boots are perfect for fall and winter. Some women wear ankle boots (booties) year-around. If you only need or want one pair, choose a boot in a neutral color that goes with the majority of your clothes. Black, brown, and tan are classic colors for boots. Higher quality boots are usually made of leather, although you may want to avoid suede if you get a lot of rain or snow.

Common styles of boots are ankle boots, Chelsea boots, cowboy boots, knee-high boots with heels, moto boots, riding boots, and wedge boots.

Ankle boots have become a classic because of their versatility. They can be dressy or casual, and can be worn with skirts, dresses, pants, and over or under jeans. Chelsea boots are a fitted ankle boot with elastic on the sides, making them easy to pull on and off. Cowboy boots have a chunky, slanted heel, and are ideal for women who like western styles. Knee-high boots with heels are a sexy style that can dress up even the most casual outfit. Moto boots are a biker boot with a low heel, and they are a great everyday boot for women who like the cool, rocker style. Riding boots are a classic low-heeled boot favored by women who prefer classic styles and the equestrian theme. Wedge boots are similar to wedge sandals and are equally comfortable to wear.

In addition to making the same choices about color, material, style, accents, and heel height that you have with other shoes, there are additional considerations when it comes to boots. With knee-high boots, you have to make sure the calf width and shaft height fit your legs. The boots should hit around an inch below the bottom of your kneecap and they should fit closely to your calf. Mid-calf boots hit at the widest part of your calf, so they are not the most flattering fit. If you choose mid-calf boots, they should be fitted but not tight or they will make your legs look wider.

If you are going to wear ankle boots with shorts, skirts, dresses, cropped jeans, or over skinny jeans, you may want shorter boots that reveal the curve of your ankle bone. Otherwise, the boot will look like it cuts off your legs, making you look shorter. If you are wearing ankle boots under straight-leg or bootcut jeans or pants, you will want them to come up over your ankle so the opening at the top of the boot does not show.

> CHECKLIST ACTION: Pick your favorite styles
> of boots. Add notes, such as preferred colors,
> materials, heel heights, etc.

Pumps

Pumps are a very versatile shoe. They are professional enough for work. They can turn a casual outfit into a dressier one. They can be a sexy shoe for date night. You can wear them for many different occasions, like parties, weddings, funerals, and other special events. They are one of the easiest shoes to wear with dresses, skirts, and pants. There are no straps, so your pants, long skirts, and long dresses will not get caught on your shoes. They are easy to slip on and off. Additionally, you can wear pumps with skinny, straight-leg, and bootcut jeans and pants. They can also be worn year-around.

Common styles of pumps are classic, kitten heel, peep toe, platform, slingback, and stiletto.

The black pointy-toe pump is the ultimate classic, but nude pumps, animal skin pumps, and those with an almond toe are also classics. Kitten heels have a lower, skinny heel, and are often worn by women who prefer classic or romantic styles. Peep-toe pumps are a little more playful than closed-toe pumps, and they are often favored by glamorous women. Slingback pumps work well for spring and summer, when you want a less covered-up look. Stilettos are a sexy pump with a very thin and very high heel, which look good but can be harder to walk in.

While black and nude pumps are classics, you can substitute other neutral colors if they are more to your liking. If you are going to have more than one pair of pumps, choose pumps that match your personality and work well with your wardrobe. If you like bright colors, a fuchsia pump may be just your thing. If you are a romantic, a floral pump may be perfect for you. If you favor a chic style, you may love leopard-print or snakeskin stilettos. You can also personalize your look through accents, like bows, cutouts, or jewels.

CHECKLIST ACTION: Pick your favorite styles of pumps. Add notes, such as preferred colors, materials, heel heights, etc.

Sneakers

Sneakers are the final shoe category. They are generally one of the most comfortable shoes you will own. Sneakers can be worn for athletic purposes, but you can also just wear them as casual footwear. What makes a sneaker a sneaker is the rubber sole, but you still have choices as to which type of sneakers you want and need.

Common styles of sneakers are lace-up low-tops, lace-up high-tops, and slip-ons. Styles can also be categorized based on whether you are wearing them for athletic purposes or just as a casual shoe.

If you are wearing sneakers for athletic purposes, you will want to find a shoe designed for that specific exercise, sport, or activity. Shoes are designed differently based on whether they are for running, walking, cross-training, hiking, skateboarding, tennis, golf, cycling, or some other purpose.

I learned this lesson the hard way in my twenties. I didn't think the shoe mattered, so I used to run on concrete sidewalks in whatever type of sneaker I had on hand. I ended up having to see a podiatrist, who told me I had damaged the bones in my feet from running without the proper shoes. I still occasionally have pain in my right foot. So I urge you to be smarter than me and wear athletic shoes designed for your sport or activity.

Nike and Adidas are two of the most popular brands for athletic shoes, but you really have to find the brand that best fits your foot. Some women swear by New Balance, and I really like Skechers GOwalk for walking.

From a style perspective, athletic shoes look best with athletic clothing. The larger soles and padding that support your feet also make the shoes bulkier. As a result, athletic shoes do not look good with non-athletic shorts, jeans, skirts, or dresses.

For the sneakers you wear to run errands or hang out, you may want to focus more on style and less on performance. Vans are the West Coast classic sneaker, and Converse are the East Coast classic sneaker. Keds are another popular sneaker.

A white leather sneaker is still a classic, but canvas shoes are also popular and allow you to introduce more colors and patterns. You can also buy designer sneakers, which may add other materials like suede, other accents like zippers, and other heel heights like the wedge.

If you are wearing sneakers for style rather than physical activities, it is best to wear no-show socks. Also, sneakers look best with shorts, casual skirts and dresses, and skinny or cropped jeans. They do not look good with longer jeans or those with any type of flare.

CHECKLIST ACTION: Pick your favorite styles of sneakers. Add notes, such as your activity or sport for athletic shoes, and your preferred colors and materials for your casual sneakers.

When you are buying shoes in your preferred styles, remember to ask yourself:

1. Do they fit?
2. Are they comfortable?
3. Do they flatter my feet?
4. Do they go with the clothes in my closet?

And maybe one more...do you love them? If you do, you can bring them home and introduce them to your clothes. Then make sure you take good care of them.

Find a good, local cobbler to reinforce soles and add heel caps to your better shoes. If you do not know a cobbler, ask a stylish friend or family member. You can also ask someone who works in a shoe store or in the shoe department of a higher-end department store like Nordstrom's.

At home, be sure to clean and polish your shoes. If rain or snow are common where you live, you may also want to weatherproof your shoes. Finally, if you have knee-high or taller boots, you may want to use rolled-up magazines, pool noodles cut to the height of the boot, or boot inserts when you are storing your boots to help them hold their shape.

Now...on to handbags.

Handbags

It is hard to believe that the original handbag was a small purse used solely for holding coins...and that men carried them as often as women. The handbag has come a long way since then. Today's handbags are still functional, but they are also a stylish accessory that helps complete your look.

Common styles of handbags are clutches, crossbody bags, evening bags, hobo bags, satchels, and totes.

Clutches are a great option for business and dressier occasions. They work best when you do not have much to carry.

Crossbody handbags are a casual bag perfect for running errands. They are also ideal for travel and outdoor activities, as they leave your hands free and are harder for a thief to snatch.

Evening bags are ideal for formal events. They are often metallic or black and may include crystals or other embellishments.

Hobo bags are a soft, slouchy bag, and are great for everyday use.

Satchels are structured handbags with a flat bottom and two short handles. They work well for business and for times when you want a more polished, classy look. A convertible satchel is one that also has a removable long strap, giving you even more options.

Totes are ideal when you have a lot to carry. They are often used for the office, for the beach, and for all the necessities of mothers with young children.

Function

When it comes to handbags, we often gravitate to style first and function second. However, if the bag does not function well, you will not use it. You may carry it a few times, but then you will switch back to the "worn-in" bag that may not look like much but serves your needs better. You can have function and style, but you need to think about your needs first.

First, think about your lifestyle needs. When you are considering buying a new handbag, ask yourself where you would wear it. If you already have three evening clutches but only attend one formal event a year…you probably do not need another clutch. Before you add any extra handbags, make sure you have the perfect bag for each of your lifestyle categories: casual, dressy casual, business, etc.

Second, think about what size handbag you need for each type of bag you carry. If you usually carry a lot of stuff with you, it does not make sense to buy a small everyday bag. You will just overstuff it – which is fine for a turkey, but not very stylish for a handbag! Rather than trying to make your stuff fit into the bag, make the bag fit your stuff.

Third, consider the features that are important to you. Do you like having an outside pocket for your cell phone? Do you like having an inside pocket for your glasses? Do you prefer a single strap shoulder bag or one with double straps? If having zippers, snaps, clasps, magnetic closures, or other features are important to you, make sure you buy a handbag that has them. If the things you grab for most often are not easily accessible, you will probably stop carrying the bag.

When a handbag catches your eye, admire it all you like, but do not actually buy it unless it meets your functional needs and will serve its intended purpose. Function first. Style second.

Style

You do not have to sacrifice style for function. You can have both, but you may have to be patient. It may take time to find the perfect bag or bags that meet your major wants and needs. What is the rush? You are better off making do with the handbags you already have than continuing to accumulate "good-enough" handbags. They will just end up in the closet keeping company with the other handbags, shoes, and clothing you do not wear...like those poor misfit toys in the *Rudolph the Red-Nosed Reindeer* movie.

When it comes to style, there are a number of different factors to consider in addition to your personal preferences.

First, consider the colors and styles of your shoes and clothing. If your clothes and shoes are mainly black, white, and gray, with pops of red, you may want to select a black handbag that will work well with everything. If your style is classic, you may want to choose a leather satchel bag for everyday use and a chain-strap quilted bag for evenings out. While black and brown leather bags are classics and work well with most clothes, your everyday bag could be any neutral color or even a neutral pattern, like snakeskin. The key is to choose a color or pattern that goes with most of your wardrobe and that you will not get tired of looking at every day.

Second, think about the strap length. Where the handbag hits your body is what will be emphasized, so a bag that hits mid-torso will emphasize your waist more than your hips. If you look in the mirror, you can see how your silhouette is affected by where the bag hits. Many straps are adjustable. If they are not, a tailor can usually shorten the strap.

Third, consider the size of the handbag. From a style perspective, the handbag should be proportional to your size. If you are larger or taller, a larger bag looks best. If you are smaller or shorter, a smaller bag looks best. Of course, size is also a functional issue. If you are a smaller woman who carries a lot of stuff, you may need a larger handbag. If downsizing your purse contents is not an option, choose function over style on this one.

Fourth, think about the shape of your bag. To achieve balance, you may want to choose a handbag shape that is different from your body shape. Straight body shapes look great with hobo bags, because they add curves. Pear body shapes look great with satchel bags, because their short straps cause the bag to hit at the waist rather than adding width at the hips. Apple body shapes look great with crossbody bags that hit at the hips, balancing out stronger shoulders. Hourglass body shapes can wear most types of handbags, but the size of the bag still needs to be proportional to your size.

Fifth, you may want to consider the seasons. In warmer months, you may want lighter colors and materials for your handbags. White and tan colors, and straw and canvas fabrics, are good options. For cooler months, you may want to switch to a darker color and heavier materials. Black, brown, and gray colors, and suede and other leather materials, are great options. Navy, gold, and silver work year-around. Leather can be worn all year as well.

Finally, when it comes to quality, it is worth investing more for your primary handbags. They will look better and last longer. If you mainly need one casual, everyday bag; one nicer, structured bag; and one evening bag, make sure those three bags are of good quality. That does not mean they have to be high-end designer bags, like Louis Vuitton. You can find high quality, leather, affordable luxury purses from brands like Coach.

Be sure to take good care of your quality bags, so they will continue to look good. Clean and polish your leather handbags, and weatherproof them if you get a lot of rain or snow. You may want to store your better bags in the fabric or felt bags that came with them. This will prevent them from drying out, getting scratches, or collecting dust.

Once you have your primary handbags, you can add other bags just for fun. If your clothing is mainly neutral, you can use your handbags to add some personality. You can add your favorite colors and patterns. You can also buy handbags with accents, like zippers, tassels, fringe, or charms. If you really want a personalized handbag, you can even upload a favorite photo to a site like Etsy and use it as your handbag design. As with all your handbags, just make sure the bag is functional, as well as stylish.

CHECKLIST ACTION: List your preferred styles of handbags for each of your lifestyle needs. Note any functional or stylish features you want, including size, color, material, compartments, etc.

Jewelry

Jewelry allows you to personalize your look, add a dash of style, and transform a bland outfit into a beautiful one. While personalization is a key part of the entire *Style & Clothing System*, it is particularly applicable to jewelry. While you can (and should) choose clothing, shoes, and handbags based on your personal preferences, there are also some restrictions. Your size, shape, features, and lifestyle all impact what type of clothes, shoes, and bags will best fit and flatter you. Jewelry gives you much more freedom to express yourself with fewer limitations. You can just be your amazing self and wear whatever pleases you.

Wearing jewelry that is personally meaningful can have a big impact on how you feel. For instance, my husband gave me an anchor pin from when he attended the Naval Academy for two years. I put it on the lapel of my denim jacket and love wearing it because it reminds me of him.

Charm bracelets are another way to wear jewelry that makes you happy. When I published my last book on fine art photography, a friend gave me a bracelet to which she had added a little camera charm. When I wear the bracelet, I think of our friendship.

There are so many ways to personalize your jewelry. You may have jewelry handed down from a family member. You may have picked up jewelry on your travels. You may have a class ring from your alma mater or a necklace with the logo of your favorite sports team. You may have jewelry with your birthstone, or the birthstones of your husband and children. You can even take a class and learn how to make your own jewelry.

Jewelry can also reflect your personal interests. If you love horses, you might like an equestrian cuff. If you love the beach, you might like a sea glass necklace. If you ride motorcycles or just like the biker look, you may want a Harley Davidson ring. You can also reflect your spiritual or religious beliefs through your choice of jewelry. No matter what your beliefs, interests, or hobbies, you can find jewelry that reminds you of the things you love. It might even be a conversation starter that allows you to meet like-minded people.

In addition to finding jewelry that is personally meaningful, you may also want jewelry that just makes you look and feel beautiful. Maybe it brings out the color of your eyes, looks beautiful against your skin, or brightens up your most neutral outfits.

While personalization is key with jewelry, do not forget the other two elements of a perfect wardrobe: versatility and style. To be versatile, you should be able to wear the jewelry with many different outfits. If you mainly wear tops with three-quarter (aka bracelet) sleeves or shorter, a tennis bracelet may be a great option for you. To be stylish, the jewelry should also make you look good. If you have a warm skin tone, a gold link necklace may be a stylish option for you. If you have a cool skin tone, you may prefer silver.

If you have jewelry that you rarely wear, it is probably not versatile, not stylish, or not a good fit for you. We make impulse buys with jewelry, just as we do with clothes, shoes, and handbags. A piece of jewelry catches our eye, and we buy it because we like it. We forget about the bigger picture. Does it look good on us, fit our style, and go with our clothes?

To help you avoid future impulse purchases, take a look at your current jewelry. What jewelry do you wear the most? Why? Does it have personal significance? Do you get compliments whenever you wear it? Is it high quality? Does it go well with most of your clothes? Does it fit your personality?

What jewelry do you wear the least? Why? Is it cheaply made? Not flattering on you? Not really your style (possibly a gift)? Not a good fit with your clothes? Not comfortable? Too hard to clasp? Or just not practical for your lifestyle?

Thinking about the reasons you wear, or do not wear, your current jewelry can help you make smarter jewelry choices in the future.

While there are many different types of jewelry, the most common types include:

- Necklaces
- Earrings
- Bracelets
- Rings

Common styles of necklaces are bibs, chains, chokers, pendants, and strands.

When choosing a necklace, consider the width of your neckline. Wider necklaces look best with wider necklines. For example, a bib necklace works well with scoop or square necklines, which expose more skin. A skinny necklace would practically disappear with a wider neckline.

Also, consider the length of your neckline. The higher the neckline, the longer the necklace can be. For instance, long necklaces work well with turtlenecks, and short necklaces work well with v-necks.

Common styles of earrings are drop, hoop, and stud.

When choosing your earrings, consider the occasion. Drop earrings, especially chandelier styles, are dressier. For hoop earrings, thinner and larger hoops are more casual than thicker, smaller hoops. Stud earrings are the most versatile and comfortable. You can wear them every day and with almost any type of outfit.

Common styles of bracelets are bangle, charm, cuff, and link.

Bracelets are great for warmer weather and any time your wrists are exposed. Choose the styles that work well with the clothing styles you wear most frequently.

Common styles of rings are band, cocktail, and stacked.

CHECKLIST ACTION: Pick your favorite styles of necklaces, earrings, bracelets, and rings. Add notes, such as your preferred metals and stones.

Other Accessories

In addition to shoes, handbags, and jewelry, there are many other accessories that can help you pull together an outfit.

Although belts are worn less frequently these days, they can give an outfit a polished, pulled-together look. They are also a great way to add a pop of color, emphasize your waist, or add details to simple clothing. Choose different colors, fabrics, accents, and widths to suit your style and clothing.

Scarves can add a stylish touch to even the most neutral outfit. Patterned silk square scarves can be tied at the neck, but they can also be worn in place of a belt or wrapped around the strap of a handbag. In addition to silk, scarves made from cashmere and wool are good choices.

Hats are a stylish way to protect you from the sun in the summer, the cold in the winter, and a bad hair day any time of the year. They can also add a stylish twist to your outfits. Hat styles to consider are fedora, panama, floppy, berets, cowboy, beanies, boater, bowler, and caps.

Sunglasses are another functional and stylish accessory. Certain styles of sunglasses work best with certain face shapes. If you have a square jaw, try curvier frames like aviator, oval, round, or butterfly. If you have a round face, try geometric frames like wayfarer, oval, or rectangle. If you have a heart-shaped face, try cat-eye, rimless, semi-rimless, or round frames. If you have an oval face, almost any frame will work. Proportion is also important, so choose the size of your sunglasses based on the size of your face.

Prescription glasses are rarely included in lists of accessories, but they should be because they are worn every day. Like sunglasses, they should fit your face shape and be proportional to your size. Your glasses should not touch your cheek, should not hide your eyebrows, and should not be wider than your face. The arms should sit comfortably on your ears and the glasses should be straight. If you only have one pair, be sure to choose a color and style that will work well with most of your clothing. Most important, keep your prescription current!

Gloves and umbrellas are additional functional accessories that can also be stylish. Black is classic for gloves and umbrellas, but you can buy yours in any color or pattern that suits your style and works well with your outerwear. You can also incorporate technology if you choose. Touch technology for gloves lets you use your smart phone without having to take off your gloves. Umbrellas with an automatic open-and-close feature are convenient.

Your shoes, handbags, jewelry, and other accessories are a key part of your look-good, feel-good wardrobe. Rather than mindlessly accumulating a large collection of mediocre items, choose each one carefully and you will end up loving and wearing them all.

Step 7

Choose Your Preferred Brands & Stores

The seventh step in the *Style & Clothing System* is to choose your go-to brands and stores. The ideal brands are those that offer good quality at an affordable price. To be perfect for you, the brands must also fit your style and body. The ideal stores are those that offer a great selection and customer-friendly policies and services.

Identifying the brands and stores that work best for you makes it easier to create and maintain your perfect wardrobe. It allows you to narrow down the huge universe of clothing, shoes, handbags, and accessories to those that fit and flatter you. Of course, you can still shop elsewhere, but it will be by choice, not necessity.

Pay attention to what looks and feels good on you. Play favorites. If you find yourself wearing a certain pair of shoes all the time, note the brand, style, and store where you purchased them. What do you like about them? If they look great, are comfortable, *and* go well with most of your clothes, you have hit the jackpot. Next time you need a similar pair of shoes, check that brand first. It will save you time and effort. It may also save you money, because you are more likely to keep wearing the shoes rather than replacing them a few months down the road.

I debated about whether to recommend specific brands and stores, since we all have different tastes and budgets. I also hesitated because brands change – quality, style, and prices can go up or down. In the end, I decided to include recommendations because I thought specific suggestions would be more helpful to you than general statements.

Having read this far, you know that the *Style &*

Clothing System emphasizes quality over quantity…but not at any price. The sweet spot is somewhere in the middle. True value is about what something is worth, not just what it costs. Spending $15 on a cheaply made top that does not look or feel good on you is not a good value. Neither is spending $500 on a top that is the same quality and style as one you could get for $50.

When you think about brands, it helps to think of them in tiers, from highest to lowest in terms of both quality and price. You can narrow down the brands you buy to those that fall within your chosen tiers.

Luxury brands. This tier includes the highest priced brands, including haute couture and designer brands. These brands bear the names of past and present fashion designers, but many of the brands are now owned by corporations. For instance, LVMH owns Louis Vuitton, Celine, Christian Dior, Donna Karan, Emilio Pucci, Fendi, Givenchy, Kenzo, Loewe, and Marc Jacobs. Kering owns Alexander McQueen, Balenciaga, Bottega Veneta, Christopher Kane, Gucci, Puma, Saint Laurent, and Stella McCartney. The higher prices are partly due to higher quality. However, the prices are also higher to cover massive marketing costs (advertising in *Vogue* is not cheap), and to contribute to corporate profits. Customers pay for the designer name. Very few of my recommendations are from this category.

Premium brands. This tier includes higher-priced brands of great quality. You will sometimes hear the brands in this category referred to as affordable luxury or contemporary brands. Contemporary brands include modern and classic styles. Tory Burch is an example of a contemporary brand. This tier also includes bridge brands, which are the lower-priced lines of the top designers. The bridge brands may include similar styles, but with less expensive fabrics and construction than the luxury brands. You can often tell the bridge brands by the labels. For instance, Michael Kors is a luxury brand; MICHAEL Michael Kors is the bridge brand. "Better" brands are also included in this tier. They are the next step up from moderate brands in terms of quality and price. Anne Klein is an example of a better brand. *Many of my recommendations are from this category.*

Moderate brands. This category includes mid-priced brands of good quality. Moderate brands provide great value and are a good place to find casual, dressy casual, and business clothing. You can find many of your essentials here, like T-shirts, blouses, jeans, dress pants, skirts, and dresses. You can also find affordable shoes, handbags, jewelry, and other accessories. It is also a great category for buying ultra casual clothing, such as sportswear and swimwear. Examples of moderate brands are Gap, Levi's, Nine West, and

INC at Macy's. *Many of my recommendations are from this category as well.*

Discount and budget brands. This category includes lower-priced brands that are often of lower quality. It includes brands sold at stores like Wal-Mart, K-Mart, and Old Navy. Additionally, it includes fast fashion brands like H&M, Forever 21, Zara, Mango, and many Target brands (Merona, Mossimo, and Xhilaration). Finally, it includes some of the brands offered at department stores like Kohl's, J.C. Penney, and Sears. You can sometimes find stylish options and good quality at these stores, but you have to look harder to find them. Since the *Style & Clothing System* is supposed to simplify your life once you put it in place, I have not included many recommendations from this category.

Off-price retailers. This category includes a variety of price points and offers a wide range of quality. It includes stores like T.J. Maxx and Marshall's, as well as outlet stores like Nordstrom Rack. I admit that I like shopping in these stores sometimes. The thrill of the hunt can be fun, and sometimes you can find good bargains. But...you have to wade through a lot of merchandise, and the quality is spotty. I had always assumed that the clothes, shoes, and handbags in these stores were just excess, unsold inventory from upscale stores. However, a *Huffington Post* article by Shannon Whitehead stated, "The reality is that outlets broker deals with designers so they can put designer labels on the cheaply made clothing manufactured in their own low-quality factories." A blog post by Chavie Lieber on *Racked* noted, "In reality, much of the merchandise at the outlets of major department stores is made or bought specifically for those outlets, with designers and vendors creating familiar-looking pieces at a lower cost that often indicates inferior quality." When shopping in off-price retailers and outlet stores, remember the earlier tips about how to spot quality fabrics and construction. I have not included recommendations from this category.

Although I am not recommending specific lower-tier brands, they may still have a place in your wardrobe. A mix of high and low can be stylish. Also, in some cases it may make sense to buy lower-tier brands. The test is how much wear you will get out of the item. If you want a sparkly dress for New Year's Eve, you may want to save your money and buy a lower-tier brand. Similarly, if heavily embellished T-shirts are trending and you really like them, go ahead and get one from a lower-tier brand. Then you will not feel bad when they go out of style again. My advice would just be to think of these brands like fast food… fine to have on occasion, but not something you want to load up on.

Brands

Although I have placed each brand in only one category, many of them sell apparel and accessories in other categories as well. Additionally, I have attempted to include brands for all different styles – classic, bohemian, glamorous, etc. – so that you can find brands that fit your style.

The brands I recommend are those that I believe offer stylish clothes and accessories at an affordable price given the quality of their products.

Clothing

Jeans
- 7 For All Mankind
- Calvin Klein
- Hudson Jeans
- J. Brand
- Joe's Jeans
- Levi's
- Lucky Brand Jeans
- NYDJ
- Paige Denim
- True Religion

Casual & Dressy Casual
- Anthropologie
- AX ARMANI EXCHANGE by Giorgio Armani

- Banana Republic
- BCBGeneration by BCBG
- Chicos
- Eileen Fisher
- Ella Moss
- Everlane (online retailer)
- Free People
- Gap
- INC International Concepts
- J. Crew
- J. Jill
- Karen Kane
- LAUREN by Ralph Lauren
- Madewell
- Nautica
- Nic + Zoe
- RACHEL by Rachel Roy
- Splendid
- Theory
- Tommy Bahama
- Tommy Hilfiger
- Topshop
- Urban Outfitters
- Vince

Dressy

- Adrianna Papell
- Eliza J
- Tadashi Shoji

Business/Office/Work

- Ann Taylor
- Brooks Brothers
- Ellen Tracy
- Talbots
- White House Black Market

Athletic Clothing

- Athleta
- Lululemon
- North Face
- Patagonia

Intimates

- Chantelle
- Hanky Panky
- Soma
- Victoria's Secret
- Wacoal

Coats

- Barbour
- Burberry
- French Connection
- London Fog

Shoes

Casual to Dressy Shoes

- Aquatalia
- Badgley Mischka
- Donald J. Pliner
- Franco Sarto
- French Sole
- Frye
- L.K. Bennett
- Minnetonka
- Nine West
- Sam Edelman
- Stuart Weitzman
- Tory Burch
- Vince Camuto

Sneakers

- Adidas
- Converse
- Keds
- Nike
- Skechers
- Vans

Handbags

- Coach
- Cole Haan
- Dooney & Bourke

- Fossil
- Kate Spade New York
- MARC by Marc Jacobs
- MICHAEL by Michael Kors
- Rebecca Minkoff

Jewelry

- Baublebar
- Chan Luu
- Dana Rebecca
- David Yurman
- Eddie Borgo
- Etsy
- Kendra Scott
- Pandora

Sunglasses

- Maui Jim
- Oakley
- Ray-Ban

CHECKLIST ACTION: Make a list of your favorite brands of clothing, shoes, handbags, jewelry, and other accessories. Add specific notes, as needed. For instance, if you like one brand for sandals, but another for flats, make a note to that effect. If you keep an updated list of your favorite brands, shopping will become much easier.

Stores

Some stores offer customer-friendly policies and services in addition to providing stylish clothing, shoes, and handbags. They may allow more time for returns, which is an added convenience for you. They may offer free shipping and returns for online purchases, which saves you money. They may also provide complimentary services, like personal shoppers who can help you build a stylish wardrobe, while saving you time, money, and effort.

Following is a list of stores that provide customer-friendly policies or services:

Athleta
- No time limit for returns if you have a receipt
- Free shipping in the U.S. with purchase of $50 or more & free returns

Bloomingdales
- Allows up to 365 days for returns
- Free shipping in the U.S. with purchase of $150 or more & free returns
- Free personal shoppers

J. Crew
- Free shipping in the U.S. with purchase of $150 or more (they deduct $5 from refunds for return shipping)
- Free personal stylists
- Free basic alterations (e.g. hemming) on full-price merchandise

Macy's
- No time limit for returns if you have a receipt
- Free shipping in the U.S. with purchase of $99 or more & free returns
- Free personal shoppers

Madewell
- Free shipping in the U.S. with no minimum purchase (they deduct $5.95 from refunds for return shipping)
- Free personal stylists
- Free hemming of jeans
- $20 credit toward a new pair of jeans when you bring in an old pair of jeans, which will be recycled into housing insulation for use by Habitat for Humanity

Nordstrom
- No time limit for returns with or without a receipt
- Free shipping in the U.S. with no minimum purchase & free returns
- Free personal stylists
- Free basic alterations on full-price merchandise
- Bra and shoe fit specialists

Von Maur
- No time limit for returns if you have a receipt
- Free shipping in the U.S. with no minimum purchase & free returns

- Some alterations are free and there is a small fee for others
- Offers an interest-free charge card for customers
- Free gift wrap

Zappos

- Allows up to 365 days for returns
- Free shipping in the U.S. with no minimum purchase & free returns
- Fast shipping, in as little as 1 business day for VIP customers (free)

TIP: Policies change over time, so be sure to confirm the store's current policy. Many stores note their shipping and return policies at the top of their website's home page or provide a link to their policy at the bottom of the page. Also, note any exceptions to the store's policy. For instance, apparently so many women were wearing a special occasion dress one time and then returning it (with obvious signs of wear), that even the most generous companies (like Nordstrom) had to adjust their return policy.

CHECKLIST ACTION: Make a list of your favorite stores. Add specific notes to remind you of where you like to shop, online and off, for clothing, shoes, handbags, jewelry, and other accessories. Also note your reasons for liking the store (e.g. they offer free shipping & returns, they carry your favorite brands, etc.)

Step 8

Put Together Outfits and Consult Style Resources as Needed

—— —— —— —— —— —— —— —— —— —— —— —— —— ——

The eighth step in the *Style & Clothing System* is to create your outfits. You can think of your clothes, shoes, and accessories as your wardrobe ingredients, and the outfits you create with them as your recipes. For the best results, it helps to know the proper way to combine your ingredients. You can simplify the process by answering a few questions, learning a few outfit techniques, and consulting style resources as needed.

The Questions

To continue the cooking analogy, your decision on what to make for dinner depends on several variables: How much time do you have to cook given the day's schedule? What are you in the mood to eat? What is the main dish you are going to prepare? To create an outfit, you can ask yourself similar questions.

I asked Grasie Mercedes, an actress and fashion blogger for *Style Me Grasie*, what drove her choices when she was creating an outfit. She responded, "When putting together an outfit, I think about my schedule that day and the mood I'm in. I usually start with one item I want to wear (e.g. my favorite pair of jeans or a new top) and work from there. Ultimately for me, it's all about looking effortless and being comfortable."

Drawing on Grasie's advice, you can ask yourself the following questions before you get dressed each day:

- What is my schedule?
- What mood am I in?
- What item do I want to build my outfit around?

We often get dressed out of habit, grabbing the same clothes without giving it much thought. If you instead take a minute to check in with yourself, you will create more stylish and functional outfits.

First, think about your schedule for the day. Doing more walking than usual? Wear comfortable shoes. Going straight from a business setting to a social function? Choose a versatile outfit that works for both, and then swap out your shoes or jewelry after work. Will you be in and out of air conditioning today? Wear something layered, and remove the top layer when you are outside.

Next, consider your mood. Feeling playful? Wear a funky necklace. Feeling down? Wear a bright-colored top to cheer you up. Tired and want to be left alone today? Wear neutrals from head to toe and oversized sunglasses. Feeling flirtatious and want to be noticed? Wear black leather pants with red stilettos. Clothing is one of our most personal possessions, so use yours to reflect...or change...your mood.

Finally, decide what item you want to build your outfit around. It can be an article of clothing, pair of shoes, favorite handbag, piece of jewelry, or some other accessory. Just pick one item you want to wear based on your schedule and mood, and let it be the starting point for everything else. Try pairing the item with something different. This is a tip I learned from my stylish friend, Susan Caito. She looks like she has on a new outfit every time I see her. Her secret is that she rarely wears the same pieces together, so it just *looks* like a new outfit each time. Try mixing up your clothes, shoes, and accessories to create different looks.

I like to think of it as Garanimals for adults. If you are not familiar with Garanimals, they are a children's clothing line. Their pairing system allows children to dress themselves, because all of the tops can be mixed and matched with all of the bottoms. Genius!

Outfit Techniques

The basic recipe for an outfit is pretty simple:

Outfit Recipe = Top + Bottom + Layering Piece + Shoes + Accessories

Sometimes, it is even simpler. A dress can replace the top and bottom, and you do not always need a layering piece or accessories.

But the devil is in the details. Just consider the top alone…

You have different styles: camisoles, tanks, T-shirts, polos, blouses, button-downs, wrap tops, tunics, henleys, cropped shirts, sweatshirts, pullovers, sweaters, etc.

You have different necklines: crewneck, v-neck, boatneck, scoop neck, turtleneck, keyhole, sweetheart, square neck, cowl neck, halter, jewel neck, etc.

You have different sleeve lengths and styles: sleeveless, short sleeve, long sleeve, three-quarter sleeves, cap sleeve, cuff sleeve, bell sleeve, etc.

You probably have a headache by now from considering all the options...and that is just for tops!

To discuss every potential outfit combination would be impossible. Fortunately, it is also unnecessary. If you want to simplify the process of pulling together a stylish outfit, you can do one of two things.

Your first option is to create your own stylish uniform and wear it all the time. That is what Steve Jobs did. He always wore a black mock turtleneck, blue jeans, and sneakers. According to *Forbes*, many other famous people have also simplified their wardrobes so they do not have to think about what to wear. *Forbes* noted that author Fran Lebowitz wears a black pantsuit with a white shirt all the time. President Barack Obama wears blue or gray suits. Fashion designer Michael Kors wears a black T-shirt and black jacket. And the list goes on. Most popular: wearing all black.

Assuming you would like a bit more variety, your second option is to learn some basic outfit techniques. Then, no matter what type of clothes, shoes, handbags, and jewelry you have in your closet, you will know how to combine them to stylish effect.

Outfit techniques that make it easier to put together an outfit:

- Choose one focal point
- Combine colors effectively
- Mix fabrics and textures
- Layer for a pulled-together look
- Properly pair shoes with clothes
- Take the mirror test

Let's take a closer look at each technique.

Choose one focal point

This technique follows the same philosophy as interior design. Interior designers tell their clients to make one feature the focal point of a room. This is the feature that grabs your attention, like a piece of art, a fireplace, or an oceanfront view. If there is no focal point, the room can look boring. If there are too many focal points, the room can look too busy.

This same principle applies to outfits. If you wear a plain top, with plain pants, with plain shoes, with a plain handbag, with no jewelry…the outfit is plain boring.

However, you can go too far the other way, too. If you wear a red-sequined top, leopard-skin pants, spiked shoes, a shiny yellow purse with zippers and studs, and statement jewelry on your neck, wrists, and ears…the outfit is a wee bit over the top.

Trying to do too much in one outfit can make it look like you are trying too hard. If the outfit also includes head-to-toe designer brands, it can also make you look like a fashion victim. We do not want that!

The key to a stylish outfit is to have one star surrounded by a great supporting cast. That does not mean the focal point has to be flashy. There are ways to create emphasis without beads, sequins, and other flashy embellishments. Your focal point could be a pattern, bright color, ruffles, grommets, scallops, ruching, zippers, cutouts, peplums, or other details. Also, the rest of the outfit does not have to be plain; it just should not compete with your focal point. Let the rest of your outfit be simple, maybe even neutral, without all the bells and whistles.

An example of how to apply this technique would be to wear a blouse with a zebra print as the focal point, paired with a solid black pencil skirt, black ankle-strap heels with subtle contrast stitching, and a dark red leather purse.

Combine Colors Effectively

There are many different ways to combine colors, but the following are some of the easier combinations to get right:

The easiest technique of all is to combine neutrals with other colors. Neutrals combine well with most colors, with the exception of colors that are too similar. For instance, white does not mix with cream, and black does not mix with dark brown. When worn together, similar colors look like a failed attempt at matching.

That is also why the monochromatic look is sometimes hard to pull off. Once when my oldest stepson was waiting for his wife outside a dressing room, he overheard a woman telling her friend that something was wrong with her outfit, but she could not figure out what it was. After listening to the two women discuss it for awhile, he finally spoke up and said, "The problem is your blacks don't match." Her black pants were a different shade than her black top. (Spoiler alert: In the next section, we will discuss mixing textures. If you wear a black top and pants in two different textures, you can pull it off even if the shades of black are slightly different.)

Following are neutral colors, with examples of colors that combine well with them, as well as some colors that clash with them:

- **Black.** Looks good with almost all colors. Try combining with white, cream, tan, teal, peach, pink, emerald green, royal blue, or yellow. Black clashes with other dark colors like dark brown and midnight blue.

- **White.** Looks good with almost all colors. Try combining with black, navy, red, khaki, pink, kelly green, turquoise, or coral. White clashes with off-white colors like cream, beige, and ivory.

- **Black & White.** Together, these two colors allow for even more color combinations, because they balance each other out. If you have tops, pants, or jackets in a black-and-white pattern, you will be able to match that piece with virtually any color item in your wardrobe.

- **Brown.** Try combining with tan, camel, beige, pink, cobalt blue, turquoise, coral, or canary yellow. Brown clashes with black.

- **Cream.** Try combining with khaki, navy, brown, lavender, teal, or orange. Cream clashes with white.

- **Gray.** Try combining with black, white, pink, lime green, ice blue, or red. Gray clashes with brown and orange.

- **Khaki.** Try combining with white, cream, olive, navy, cornflower blue, pink, coral, black, or plum. Khaki clashes with tan.

- **Navy.** Try combining with white, red, yellow, tangerine, olive, or emerald green. Navy clashes with black.

- **Olive.** Try combining with navy, black, brown, cream, and white. Olive clashes with yellow and bright greens.

- **Color of blue jeans.** Try combining with white, black, and almost every other color except those that are too close to the color of the jeans.

There are far too many shades, hues, and tones to list them all, but you can use the guidelines above to get a feel for what colors combine well. When you are choosing colors to go with your neutrals, keep in mind which colors flatter your skin tone.

Another color combination technique that works well is pairing light and dark shades of the same color. A light blue top looks great with a dark blue skirt. A light gray top combines well with dark gray pants. You can even pair blue denim tops and bottoms, as long as they are in light and dark shades. For instance, a chambray button-down top looks good with a dark blue pair of jeans.

You can also find great color combinations by looking at colors that are together in nature. The blue and green shades of the ocean look pretty worn together. The orange, red, and yellow colors of the sun make a great color combination. The brown, orange, yellow, and red colors of leaves as they change colors in the fall also combine well.

Yet another color combination technique is to mix colors in the same color family. For instance, wear pastels with other pastels. Wear jewel tones with other jewel tones. Wear earth tones with other earth tones.

Finally, you can use the colors in prints to create outfits. Let's say you have a top with a navy, white, and tangerine print. You could obviously wear that top with navy or white or tangerine pants. However, you could also use the print to trigger other outfit ideas, like pairing a tangerine top with navy pants.

CHECKLIST ACTION: Make a note of your favorite color combinations.

Mix Fabrics and Textures

A technique that makes your outfits more visually appealing is to mix fabrics and textures. Wearing a cotton shirt with a cotton skirt is fine, but if you instead wear a cotton shirt with a suede skirt, the look gets more interesting.

We have previously discussed fabrics, so let's take a minute to talk about textures. Texture is what you can actually see and feel. A fabric's thickness and appearance determine its texture. Examples of different textures are fuzzy, soft, shiny, furry, rough, smooth, crisp, sheer, and bulky.

Some possible fabric and texture combinations:
- Cotton top + Denim bottom
- Silk top + Leather bottom
- Cotton top + Velvet bottom
- Suede top + Denim bottom
- Cashmere top + Leather bottom
- Linen top + Denim bottom

- Cotton top + Wool bottom
- Silk top + Wool bottom
- Cotton top + Tweed bottom
- Fuzzy top + Smooth bottom
- Soft top + Rough bottom
- Shiny top + Dark bottom
- Furry top + Smooth bottom
- Sheer top + Dark bottom

Try some different fabric and texture combinations to see which ones you like best. Do not be afraid to stray outside your comfort zone and try different looks.

Layer for a Pulled-Together Look

Layering your clothes gives you a more polished, pulled-together look. What you layer over your clothes can change your look, from casual to business to dressy. Layering also adds warmth when you need it. As a bonus, it can also help you hide those extra five pounds you put on over the holidays!

The layering piece can be a blazer, jacket, sweater, vest, top, or any other piece that can be worn over another wardrobe piece.

A guideline to make layering easy and stylish:

The first layer should be the lightest weight and the most fitted piece. The first layer could be a cami, shell, button-down shirt, blouse, thin sweater, dress, etc.

TIP: It is easiest to layer over a sleeveless or long-sleeve first layer. Shorter sleeves can show through or bunch up under the second layer.

The second layer should be in a different color or pattern. If the first layer had a pattern, the second layer should be a solid. If the first layer was solid, the second layer can either be a pattern or a solid in a different color. For maximum style, the second layer should have a different texture than the first. The second layer should also be looser and thicker. However, if you are going to add a third layer, the second layer should still be fairly light and fitted so it does not add bulk. The second layer could be a shirt, vest, sweater, jacket, blazer, etc.

The third layer should be in a solid color if either the first or second layer had a pattern. If the first two layers were solids, the third layer can have a pattern. The third layer should be the thickest and least fitted piece. If you are going to have three layers, the easiest way to pull it off is to have the first and third layer be neutrals. The third layer is generally a sweater, jacket or blazer, though it could also be a coat.

In a nutshell, the key to layering is to move from thinnest to thickest, from most fitted to least fitted, and from solid-to-patterned or solid-to-solid.

An example of three-layer dressing is to wear a button-down top as the first layer, a vest for the second layer, and a blazer for the third layer.

Properly Pair Shoes with Clothes

Pairing the right shoes with the rest of your outfit is more of an art than a science. However, there are some techniques that can help you get this one right.

If you want to wear flats with jeans, they are best paired with skinny or straight-leg jeans. The jeans should fall at or above the ankle. If the jeans are longer, you can cuff them. You want to avoid having your jeans bunch up at the bottom.

Bootcut and other flared jeans do not work well with flats. Either they drag on the ground, or they are too short and look like they shrunk in the dryer. Bootcut jeans work best with boots, pumps, or sandals with heels.

If you want to tuck your jeans into your boots, the jeans need to have a slim fit. For ankle boots, this is even more important, and a skinny fit is best. If you wear jeans with a wider leg opening, the jeans will bunch up and may even come untucked. Either you will be constantly fidgeting with them, or you will just give up and walk around with your jeans half-tucked.

If you want to wear your jeans over your boots, the jeans need to be a wider fit. If the jeans are a skinnier fit, you will be able to see the outline of the boots through your jeans. Bootcut jeans are ideal for wearing over boots. Brilliant observation, right? If there is external hardware or other accents on the sides of the boot, the boots are meant to be seen, not hidden under your jeans.

If you are wearing skirts, dresses, or shorts that are knee-length or shorter, you can wear them with flats. If your clothes go past your knees, you need a little heel height. Otherwise, the outfit is out of proportion and can look frumpy or sloppy.

If you are wearing sandals with straps around your legs or ankles, the straps should show. In other words, the hem of your pants, skirt, or dress should hit somewhere above the straps. If your hems are longer, they may get caught on the straps. They may also cover up the straps, ruining the line of the shoe. If necessary, cuff your pants to keep them above your straps.

When wearing pants with heels, shoes look best when they are proportional to the size of the leg opening. Skinny kitten heels or stilettos look good with pants that are tapered at the ankle. Chunky shoes look good with flared pants.

If you are wearing dress pants, the hem should fall about one-half inch from the ground. This is short enough that the pants will not drag on the ground, but long enough that the pants just graze the top of your shoe.

In general, the lower and thicker the heel, the more casual the shoe will make your outfit look. The higher and thinner the heel, the dressier (and sexier) the shoe will make your outfit look. This applies to sandals, boots, and shoes in general.

Take the Mirror Test

The quickest way to develop an eye for picking out great outfits is to do the mirror test. It takes less than a minute. When you have put on your *entire* outfit...clothes, shoes, jewelry, handbag, etc...take one last look in a full-length mirror before walking out the door. (If you do not have a full-length mirror, you can get one that hangs on the back of a door for as little as $15 at Target.)

When you look in the mirror, check your overall look. Giving yourself a hard time or criticizing your *perceived* flaws is not allowed. Just check your outfit. Shoes look good with the outfit? Color combinations working okay? Outfit look like it needs something, maybe a blazer to pull everything together? Outfit look like it needs to lose something, like too much jewelry?

If anything looks off, make a quick change. If you do not have time to make the change, then at least make a mental note for next time.

The problem for most of us is not that we cannot figure out if an outfit is working, it is that we never take the time to look. We get dressed in a hurry, throw on our shoes at the last minute, and grab our handbag as we head out the door. Slow down. My husband sometimes reminds me of the Navy SEALs saying, "Slow is smooth; smooth is fast." Take a breath. Glance at yourself in the mirror. Then smile, because you know you look great!

NOTE: I am not kidding about the smile. If you smile at yourself in the mirror, you will get your day started on a positive note. It produces happiness, and it only takes a second. There is even scientific evidence to show it works. In an article for *How Stuff Works*, Julia Layton discussed a study on the emotional effect of smiling published by psychologist Robert Zajonc. His study showed that the facial changes involved in smiling directly impact brain activities associated with happiness. That should give you something to smile about!

Style Resources

Just as a cook must sometimes consult a cookbook, it helps to have style resources that you can consult for outfit ideas. These resources can help you develop your own sense of style. They can also help you with specific questions. For instance, some resources can give you ideas about what to wear with clothes and shoes you already own. Some can help you pick out your next wardrobe purchase...and even buy it. Others can help you decide what to wear for specific events or occasions, like a gallery opening or a friend's tropical wedding.

Anything or anyone could potentially be a style resource, but I believe you will find the following resources especially helpful.

Style Blogs

While many style blogs focus on current trends, others focus on lasting style with a dash of trends thrown in. Following are some style blogs worth checking out. Their styles vary, so you will likely find at least one that appeals to you. Keep in mind that style blogs come and go, so if one is no longer active by the time you read this, check out the others.

- *Alterations Needed* at www.alterationsneeded.com
- *Eat.Sleep.Wear* at www.eatsleepwear.com
- *Happily Grey* at www.happilygrey.com
- *Harper and Harley* at www.harperandharley.com
- *Kendi Everyday* at www.kendieveryday.com
- *Mama in Heels* at www.mamainheels.com

- *NOA//NOIR* at www.noanoir.com
- *Style Me Grasie* at www.grasiemercedes.com
- *The Fashion Guitar* at www.thefashionguitar.com
- *Who What Wear* at www.whowhatwear.com

Other Online Style Resources

When it comes to style, the most helpful websites are those that include images of outfits. Pictures of individual wardrobe pieces are helpful when you are shopping, but seeing an entire outfit is more helpful when you are trying to decide what to wear. The following resources allow you to see individual clothes, shoes, and handbags, *and* complete outfits.

Pinterest. I like Pinterest for finding outfit ideas. You can search for ideas based on occasion, season, style, color...pretty much anything. For instance, if you are thinking of getting ankle boots but are not sure what you want, you can go to www.pinterest.com and search on "ankle boots" to get some ideas. If you already have the boots but want to know what to wear with them, you can search on "ankle boots outfit." You can be as specific as you like, such as typing in "black ankle boots" or "winter ankle boots outfit."

If you like several images posted by the same person, you can follow them or their board. For instance, I set up a board called "Style & Clothing Images" with outfits I like. If you want to check out the board, you will see examples of the principles I have discussed in this book: https://www.pinterest.com/karadlane/style-clothing-images/.

Polyvore. Polyvore is the world's largest style community. If you go to www.polyvore.com, you can not only browse for your wardrobe needs, but you can also make a purchase if you find something you want and need. (But the earlier advice about avoiding impulse buys still applies.) The products vary from affordable to luxury items, but you can narrow down your options by price.

In addition to looking for individual wardrobe pieces, you can also use Polyvore's "Outfits" feature. If you click on "Outfits," you can select from the default options like "work wear," "spring," "casual," "boho," "street style," etc. You can also just type in your own search. This feature lets you look for outfits that fit your style and for ideas on what to wear for various occasions or events.

Websites of your favorite brands or stores. Another great resource for finding outfit ideas is to visit the websites of your favorite brands and stores. You already buy from them, so use their websites to see suggested ways to wear your purchases. A few websites I particularly like for outfit ideas are J. Crew, Madewell, and Nordstrom.

Fashion Magazines

If you ignore the more extreme fashion spreads and ads in the fashion magazines, you can find helpful style information. For instance, *InStyle* has a regular feature called *Instant Style* that helps women find the styles that work for them. It shows numerous outfits, each with a different focal point. For example, they might show outfits with striped T-shirts or dresses with bows. *Harper's Bazaar* has a section called *The List*, which shows various wardrobe pieces, along with stylist's tips on how to wear them. They also have a section called *The Bazaar*, with each page featuring wardrobe pieces with a different theme, such as "free spirit." The other fashion magazines also offer helpful information, outfit ideas, and tips. Following are the top fashion magazines:

- *Allure*
- *Elle*
- *Glamour*
- *Harper's Bazaar*
- *InStyle*
- *Marie Claire*
- *StyleWatch*
- *Vogue*

Flip through a few magazines at the store or library to see which ones appeal to you. If you find any you like, you may want to subscribe to them. It is much cheaper than buying them at a newsstand. One caveat though. The advertisers in the magazines obviously want you to buy the wardrobe pieces they are advertising. Stick with what we have been discussing in the *Style & Clothing System* and only buy what makes you look and feel good.

Style Icons

You can also come up with outfit ideas by looking to style icons for inspiration. Your icons could be actresses, models, artists, musicians, business women, or anyone else whose style you like. It does not have to be a celebrity. It could be your mom, sister, friend, or someone else you know.

Remember to separate the look from the person. Icons are great for style inspiration and coming up with outfit ideas, but you still want to focus on what works for you. If you see a look you like, you can always personalize it to make it your own.

Style icons from the past include women like Audrey Hepburn, Grace Kelly, and Jackie Kennedy Onassis. Their styles were truly timeless. If you are looking for more contemporary style icons, consider the women below. If you are unsure of their styles, you can use

Pinterest or Google Images to give you a visual. Just enter the style icon's name + "style."

- Amal Clooney
- Blake Lively
- Carla Bruni Sarkozy
- Carolina Herrera
- Charlotte Gainsbourg
- Gwyneth Paltrow
- Jamie Chung
- Jennifer Aniston
- Jennifer Lopez
- Kate Moss
- Kate Upton
- Olivia Palermo
- Reese Witherspoon
- Sarah Jessica Parker
- Sofia Coppola
- Taylor Swift
- Victoria Beckham
- Zoe Saldana

TIP: To help develop your personal style, you may want to create your own lookbook. Fashion designers use lookbooks to display and market their latest collections, but you can use one to collect images that appeal to you. As you see images you like, you can cut them out or print them off and paste them into a scrapbook or notebook. The images could be of an individual wardrobe piece or an entire outfit. Also consider images other than clothing. An image of a color you like, the ocean, a work of art, architecture, or anything that appeals to you can be a source of wardrobe inspiration. I created a lookbook, and it has helped me to figure out my style. If you prefer, you can also use Pinterest to set up an online version of a lookbook.

CHECKLIST ACTION: Choose your favorite style resources.

Like anything else, pulling together great outfits takes practice. There is no rush, and you can learn as you go through trial and error.

You will have more fun experimenting if you do not take it too seriously. If you try a look that does not work out, it is not fatal. The world will go on. After all, we are talking about clothes here, not finding a solution to global issues!

Step 9

Analyze, Declutter, and Organize Your Wardrobe

- – – – – – – – – – – – – – –

T he ninth step in the *Style & Clothing System* is to analyze, declutter, and organize your wardrobe. Analyzing your wardrobe means taking stock of what you currently own. Decluttering means getting rid of the wardrobe pieces that do not fit you, flatter you, or work with your lifestyle. Organizing means setting up a system for your current and future wardrobe.

At the beginning of this book, I mentioned that the average woman only wears 20 percent of her wardrobe. You no longer have to be one of those average women. You know how to create a versatile, stylish, personalized wardrobe that you will love wearing. You also know how to pull the pieces of your wardrobe together to create great outfits. There is just one minor detail we have not discussed: What do you do about your current wardrobe?

Knowing what to do going forward is helpful, but you still have to start with your current wardrobe. That is actually a good thing. I once had to start from scratch. If that sounds like a dream come true, believe me it was not. A number of years ago, there was a gas line explosion in my neighborhood. It damaged over eighty homes and completely destroyed six. Mine was one of the six. I lost nearly everything in the fire except my car and the clothes I wore to work that day. The only good thing that came out of the experience is that it taught me what was important in life. Material possessions are nice, but I no longer value them as much as I once did.

On a lighter note, Murphy's Law was in full force and effect that day. What I had on at the time was my *least* favorite dress. So I had a wardrobe that consisted of one dress that I did not even like. On the bright side, I was wearing 100 percent of my clothes!

Even if you wanted to, you could not buy a completely new wardrobe all at once. If you do not believe me, try buying summer clothing when stores are rolling out their fall clothing lines. Besides, just because you go shopping does not mean you will find what you want. It is hard enough to accumulate a wardrobe full of clothes you love over time; trying to do it all at once is mission impossible. I had to settle for buying good-enough clothing after the fire, but you do not have to settle. You can work with the clothes you have until you find the ones you really want.

So let's get to work analyzing your current wardrobe, then decluttering and organizing your closets and drawers.

Analyze Your Current Wardrobe

I previously noted I had analyzed my closets and drawers and found I had 604 items in my wardrobe. Your turn. If you have time and are detail-oriented, you can set up a spreadsheet to record everything, like I did. (Did I mention I was a CPA?) For instance, I included a breakdown of all my tops by color, sleeve length, and style (T-shirts, turtlenecks, etc.), and then noted how many of each item I owned. If you are time-pressed or that just sounds like *way* too much work, you can simplify the process by taking the following steps:

First, grab a pad of paper and a pen…and a cup of coffee, bottle of water, glass of wine, or whatever your beverage of choice happens to be. On the pad of paper, list the following categories (or modify them to suit you):

Tops, Shirts & Blouses _____
Sweaters _____
Total Tops _____

Jeans _____
Pants _____
Skirts & Shorts _____
Dresses _____
Total Bottoms _____

Jackets _____
Blazers _____
Total Layering Pieces _____

Flats _____
Sandals _____
Boots _____
Pumps _____
Sneakers _____
Total Shoes _____

Total Handbags _____

GRAND TOTAL _____

For extra credit, you can also add bras and panties, workout clothes, swimwear, coats, and any other clothing, shoes, jewelry, or accessories.

Second, go through your closets and drawers, count how many of each item you have, and write it down.

There are two ways you can do this. One, you can pick a category, like sweaters, and go through and count those first. Then write down that number and move on to the next category. If you are going to do this in stages, I would recommend this method.

However, if you are going to do this all at once, you can instead go through your closets from left to right and your drawers from top to bottom and just use hash marks to count each item as you come to it. The benefit is that you only touch each item once. If the first three items in your closet are jackets, put three hash marks next to that category. If the fourth item is a dress, put one hash mark next to that category. Just keep going, putting a slash through each fifth hash mark to make it easier to tally the totals at the end. I used this method, and it took me about an hour to count everything even using more detailed categories.

Third, add everything up to see how many tops, bottoms, layering pieces, shoes, and handbags you have. Write it all down on the pad of paper.

Were you surprised by the results? Did any categories seem abnormally high to you? If so, think about the reasons. In the introduction, we talked about many of the reasons we end up with clothes we do not wear. Do any of those reasons help to explain why some of your counts were so high?

In just three steps, you now have your current wardrobe count. This gives you a good starting point. However, it is not your optimal wardrobe count, because it includes all your clothes, shoes, and handbags, not just the ones you actually wear.

> TIP: You may want to do the wardrobe analysis right after putting away your laundry or picking up your dry cleaning, so you do not leave anything out of your count.

Declutter Your Wardrobe

The point of the decluttering process is to narrow down your wardrobe to only the items that fit you, flatter you, and work with your lifestyle. You can simplify and beautify your wardrobe by clearing out the clutter. It also makes getting dressed easier, because you will be able to see everything you have. So to get you to the point where you are wearing and loving 100 percent of your wardrobe, let's start decluttering.

The decluttering process can be time-consuming, so it helps to prepare in advance. If you figure out beforehand where you will take the wardrobe items that need to be altered, repaired, sold, or donated, you will save time later.

It also makes sense to decide in advance when you will do the decluttering. If you are able to block off most of a day to do it, that is the ideal option. It is more efficient and gives you the satisfaction of crossing decluttering off your list. However, if that is not possible, choose one wardrobe category at a time (e.g. tops or shoes), and block off enough time to finish that category in one sitting.

Ready to declutter?

First, grab the pad of paper where you tallied up your wardrobe count by category. We are going to use those same categories here. Go in whatever order you would like. You can start from the top (tops, shirts & blouses) and work your way down (handbags). You can start with the category where you have the least items, and work your way up to the category where you have the most items. You can do the opposite and go from the category with the most items to the one with the least. Whatever works best for you.

Second, take all of the items for your chosen category out of your closets and drawers. (For the hanging items, an alternative is to leave them hanging but move them all to one side of the closet so they are all together, making it easier for you to go through them).

Separate all of the wardrobe items into two categories: **Keep or Delete**.

The keep category is reserved for clothes that fit your body and lifestyle. These clothes make you look and feel good. They are of good quality and are in good condition. You wear them when they are in season. They also fit with your style and clothing preferences. For instance, if you have decided to stick to neutral colors and other colors that flatter your skin tone, then only clothes that meet that criteria would go into the keep category. Finally, if it is something you love, keep it...period.

The delete category includes everything else. These are clothes that do not fit or flatter you. They are clothes that are not your style or that you just do not like. They may be in poor condition, such as being faded, stained, or falling apart. They might be uncomfortable. They may be clothes that do not go with anything else in your closet. They are clothes that you rarely wear, even when they are in season. Basically, these are the clothes that are just taking up space.

In a nutshell, the keep category is for clothes you would like to keep in your versatile, stylish, personalized wardrobe. The delete category is for everything else.

Do not panic if you have more items to delete than keep. Remember that the average woman only wears 20 percent of her wardrobe, so it makes sense if you have more to delete than to keep. In addition, just because something is in the delete pile does not mean you have to get rid of it right now. You may want to get rid of some things now, and others as you can replace them. More about that shortly.

Third, record the number of keep and delete items on your pad of paper. For example, if you had previously written that you had 100 tops, you might now note that 40 are keeps and 60 are deletes. Now, we are getting somewhere. If you thought your top count seemed high before, now you know why. Only 40 percent of your tops were keepers, and the rest needed to be discarded or replaced. So you can now tell that your optimal number of tops is between 40 and 100. Since you probably were not wearing 60 of your tops anyway, you probably need closer to the 40. Even that number may be high, since you will need fewer wardrobe items as you implement the *Style & Clothing System*.

Fourth, put all the wardrobe items from the keep category back into your drawers and closets. We will organize them later, but for now just put them away.

Fifth, go through everything in the delete category and put it into one of these piles:

- Alter
- Sell
- Donate
- Replace

Alter: If the only reason you put an item in the delete category is because it does not fit, you may be able to get it altered. We talked about alterations in Step 4. Consider doing simple alterations, like hemming pants. Of course, if the item has other issues, like it is stained or cheap, it is not worth getting altered.

This pile also includes anything needing simple repairs, like buttons replaced or shoes resoled. Again, a repair is only worth doing if the item would otherwise go in the keep category.

To save time, be sure you have already pre-selected the tailor you will use for altering or repairing clothes and the cobbler you will use for shoe repairs. As we discussed earlier, you can ask others for recommendations if you do not already have a place in mind.

Sell: You may be able to sell items you no longer want if they are better quality brands. The items need to be in good condition and still be in style (another good reason to buy classic pieces that never go out of style).

A local consignment store is probably your best option. Contact a few in your area and ask them what items they are accepting and what resells well. For instance, the consignment shop I have used locally only accepts what is currently in season. They told me tops do better than pants, athletic wear also does well, and handbags make the most money. They also told me which brands resell best. Not coincidentally, many of those same brands are on my recommended list. Be sure to ask about their process. For example, at the store I have used, the seller gets 50 percent of the selling price if clothing is brought in on hangers, but only 40 percent if it is not.

Online consignment stores are another option. Some to consider are www.thredup.com, www.therealreal.com, www.poshmark.com, and www.ebay.com/s/valet. I have not used any of these, but have read and heard good things about them.

Donate: If you prefer, you can also donate your wardrobe items to charity. This is also an option for any items not suitable for resale, such as those that are out of style, not in optimal condition, or of a lower quality. Goodwill, the Salvation Army, Dress for Success, and many other charities accept used clothing.

Check to see what items the charity accepts. They often provide guidelines on their website. Some charities, like Goodwill, accept everything even if it is not in salable condition. They dispose of the clothing in other ways. For example, some Goodwill stores recycle old clothing scraps into cleaning cloths for industrial buyers.

Your donations may be tax-deductible, if you itemize your deductions. Check with your tax accountant or go to www.irs.gov and search on "charitable contributions."

Replace: This category is for wardrobe items you still wear, but would like to replace. This is clothing that is "good enough" but not exactly what you want. You wear it because you already have it and it fills a need.

For instance, you may have a navy blazer that is not ideal. You wear it anyway because you want a navy blazer, and it is the only one you have. Do not get rid of it until you find one that is perfect for you. Holding on to the blazer will remind you that it needs to be replaced. It will also keep you from buying another one that is also just "okay." Once you find the ideal navy blazer, you can sell or donate your old one.

You can put the clothes you want to replace back in your closets and drawers, but I would suggest you find a way to separate them from the clothes you want to keep. One way you can do this is to physically separate them. For instance, you can put them in a separate closet or drawer. If that is not an option, you can just move them off to the left or right side in your current closets or drawers. This will be a visual reminder to re-place them, but you will still have easy access to them.

Another thing you can do for your hanging clothes is use special hangers to designate what you want to keep, and put your to-be-replaced items on different hangers. This is what I ended up doing. I created a hanger system to fit me and to conform to my *Style & Clothing System* preferences. Read the following de-scription of the hanger system and decide if something similar would work for you.

The Hanger System:
- Decide your optimal number of tops, bottoms, and layering pieces
- Buy that number of special hangers for each category
- Only hang the clothing in your "keep" category on these hangers
- Hang everything else on whatever hangers you already have

I gave some thought to what would be the optimal number of tops, bottoms, and layering pieces to have in my closet. Keep in mind that this does not include anything that is folded and put into drawers...just the hanging stuff.

I went to the Container Store and bought 54 hangers for my tops (some acrylic hangers, some white padded hangers). I also bought 18 white wooden hangers for my bottoms (some with ribbed bars, some with clips). This was in keeping with my desire to have a 3-to-1 ratio of tops to bottoms. Finally, I bought 6 white heavier wooden hangers for my blazers and jackets.

Here is the interesting part. Despite all my clothes, I was not able to use all my new hangers right off the bat. I had bought 78 new hangers, but I did not have enough clothes that met my new requirements to use them all. Rather than moving some of my "replace" items into the "keep" category, I left some of the hangers empty. I would rather wait to find the perfect replacement pieces worthy of my new hangers!

Sixth, do not put the items you plan to alter, repair, sell, or donate back into your closets and drawers...not even temporarily. They will end up staying there and getting mixed in with your other clothing. Then all the decluttering work you did will be for naught.

Instead, put these piles somewhere out of the way until you have worked through all your wardrobe categories. Then you can just make one trip and drop off the items needing alterations or repairs at your tailor or cobbler, the items to be sold at your consignment store, and the items to be donated at your charity of choice.

> CHECKLIST ACTION: Plan the date when you will do your decluttering. Decide in advance where you will alter, repair, sell, or donate your clothes.

Organize Your Wardrobe

When it comes to organizing your wardrobe, simpler is better. You are unlikely to stay organized if the process is too complex. You also have to consider three factors: your physical space, your budget, and the number and type of items in your wardrobe.

Organizing Your Closets

Ideally, your clothes should be on hangers that are 1-inch apart. This allows your clothes to breathe, prevents wrinkles, and makes it easier for you to see what you have.

If the physical space in your closet does not allow for 1-inch spacing, you have several options. You can fold some clothes that you would otherwise hang. You can move some of your clothes to another closet. You can hire a company like California Closets or TCS Closets (part of The Container Store) to customize your closet, if you have the budget for it. Or you can further declutter until the number of items you have in your wardrobe will allow for the 1-inch spacing.

Of course, you could also just ignore the 1-inch rule, but you will lose the benefits discussed above. Your closet will be a source of stress, rather than an oasis of calm.

In terms of organizing your closets, consider the recommendations of Debbie Mikulla, the owner of Closet Control. She notes that her closet organizing service is a collaborative effort with each client, but she generally recommends that clients:

- Organize by category first: jackets, tops, pants, etc.
- Then organize by sleeve length from shortest to longest
- Then organize by color from lightest to darkest

The determination of what to hang in your closets versus fold in your drawers depends on your personal preferences, your physical space, and the types of clothing you own.

I personally prefer to hang as much as possible, since it cuts down on wrinkles and makes it easier to see what I have when getting dressed. If you would like to hang more but do not have the space, consider getting a double-hang rod. Stores like Lowe's carry them, and they double your space for tops, skirts, and pants.

The type of clothing you own also makes a difference. If you own a lot of cashmere and delicate knits, many experts advise folding them to avoid stretching them out. However, I hang many of my cashmere sweaters on padded hangers and have never had a problem.

Costume designer Alison Freer recommends hanging *everything* in her great book, *How to Get Dressed*. She even suggests you hang bras and underwear. While I would not go quite that far, I do agree with her that "… if you can't clearly see it, you aren't ever going to wear it."

Space permitting, I would recommend that you hang the following clothing:

- Blazers
- Dresses
- Jackets
- Jeans
- Pants
- Skirts
- Tops – possible exceptions are turtlenecks, bulky sweaters, cashmere sweaters, and delicate knits (if you are concerned about them stretching out)

The types of hangers depend on your clothes, preferences, and physical space. The only thing every expert agrees on is that you should not use wire hangers. Beyond that, your primary choices are acrylic, non-slip, padded, plastic, and wood. You can also get hangers with bars or clamps for jeans, pants, or skirts, and notches on the arms for strappy tops or dresses.

I previously talked about hangers in "The Hanger System" section and in the "Care" section of Step 5. You can also go to a site like The Container Store to decide what type of hangers to buy. Currently, when you go to www.containerstore.com and enter "hangers" in the search box, you will see a featured video on "How to Choose the Right Hanger."

The simplest way to organize your shoes is by category: flats, sandals, pumps, sneakers, and boots. This will make it easy for you to see your options when looking for the right shoes for your outfit. It will also make it obvious if your shoe count is a bit high in some categories...like having 20 pairs of sneakers. If you want to fine-tune your organizing even further, you could arrange your shoes by color or heel height within each category.

If you do not have custom closets with built-ins for your shoes, there are many options for organizing your physical space. You can buy cedar shoe racks for the floor of your closet. You can put your shoes on the top shelf of your closet. You can use stacking crates or clear shoe boxes or bins. You can put hanging shoe racks on the back of your closet door. You can even leave your shoes in the boxes they came in, but remove the lids and put them under the boxes so you can see the shoes. The most important thing is to make sure your shoes are visible, so you can see your options when getting dressed.

A simple way to organize your handbags is by size. By default, this generally ends up organizing them by style as well. Your evening bags tend to be the smallest, and your totes the largest. Depending on how many handbags you own, you may want to sort your bags by color as well.

Some of the same options for displaying your shoes will also work for your handbags. You can put them on the top shelf of your closet, using dividers if you choose. You can also put them in stacking crates or clear bins. You can leave your nicer handbags in the fabric or felt bags they came in. This will prevent them from getting dusty or scratched. This option works well as long as you do not have too many handbags... since the fabric or felt bags hide your handbags from view.

For belts, you can get a belt hanger or roll them and keep them in clear boxes. For scarves, you can get a scarf holder or store them in clear boxes. For hats, you can store them similarly to shoes and handbags – on shelves, in crates, or in bins.

If you do not keep your jewelry in a jewelry box, armoire, or drawer, you can keep it in your closet. You can buy hanging jewelry organizers at places like Bed, Bath & Beyond, The Container Store, or Amazon. These organizers provide separate compartments for earrings, bracelets, necklaces, and rings. You can also use a trick recommended by closet organizer Debbie Mikulla. She bought a corkboard from OfficeMax and had it framed. It hangs on the wall of her closet with pushpins to hold each of her necklaces. This arrangement allows her to see all of her necklaces at a glance, making it easier to choose one for each outfit.

Organizing Your Drawers

While hanging your clothes is usually optimal, folding them and putting them in drawers is sometimes a better option. This is particularly true if the items are smaller or if you have space limitations in your closet.

Do not overstuff your drawers. If you have to push down your clothes to close the drawer, you have too many things in the drawer. You can move some of them to another drawer. You can hang some of them. Or you can declutter further. If you overstuff your drawers, you can pretty much guarantee your clothes will be wrinkled. It will also be harder to see what you have just by opening the drawer.

I would recommend the following clothing be folded and put into drawers:

- **Tops.** Any tops you do not hang can be folded and organized in your drawers by category: tanks, T-shirts, sweaters, etc. Whether you can dedicate an entire drawer to each category depends on how much space you have and how many items you have per category. If you do not have or need an entire drawer for a category, stack your clothing by category within the drawer. Always put the heaviest tops with the longest sleeves on the bottom, so they will not crush your lighter tops.

- **Shorts.** Organize your denim shorts into one stack or drawer, since they are generally heavier than other types of shorts. Arrange your remaining shorts by color or length, whichever works best for you.

- **Bras & Panties.** If you have room, keep your bras and panties in separate drawers. Arrange bras from lightest to darkest. Some people will fold a bra in half and tuck one cup into another. To protect bras with wires, I prefer to just clasp the bra shut and leave the bra unfolded and turned sideways in the drawer. Each bra cuddles against the next one, conserving space. For panties, arrange by style (thongs, bikinis, boy shorts, etc.) and then from lightest to darkest.

- **Lingerie.** If space permits, keep your lingerie in one drawer, with separate stacks for your sexy lingerie and whatever you sleep in (assuming they are not one and the same).

- **Socks.** Keep your socks, tights, and hose in a separate drawer. For the other categories of clothing, you really do not need drawer dividers. They take up too much room, and stacks are enough to divide the clothes. The exception is the sock drawer. I keep 4 clear plastic boxes (no lids) inside my sock drawer, one each for white athletic socks, black athletic socks, dress socks, and tights & hose. After doing laundry, I ball up my socks, placing one inside the other and tossing them into the appropriate box. You can find bins of all shapes and sizes to fit your drawers.

- **Activewear.** Keep all your workout clothes in one drawer, separate from other clothing. If you have the room, you could even keep your athletic socks here, rather than in your sock drawer.

- **Swimwear.** Keep all swimwear together in one drawer, with separate stacks for bikinis, one-piece swimsuits and tankinis, and cover-ups.

The above organizing suggestions can be modified to suit your needs and preferences. For instance, if you only have six pairs of shorts, there is no need to arrange them by type, color, or length. The point is to make it as easy as possible for you to see what you have when you are getting dressed. It is also to ensure the lowest possible maintenance. For example, hanging your clothes whenever possible and not overstuffing your drawers avoids wrinkles, and therefore the need for ironing or steaming.

A common suggestion by many experts is to switch out your clothing by season. You may choose to do this if you have more wardrobe pieces than you have room for in your primary closet and drawers. The reason I did not suggest this is that the *Style & Clothing System* emphasizes seasonless clothing, through the use of layering and versatile wardrobe pieces. It also focuses on reducing the amount of clothing you need. As a result, the system is geared towards making it possible to wear most of your clothing year-around. Therefore, it is better to have all of your clothing available in your primary closet and drawers.

CHECKLIST ACTION: Plan the date when you will organize your closets and drawers.

Before we sign off on this step, I want to discuss how to *keep* your wardrobe decluttered and organized. Initially, you are motivated to keep everything nice and neat, but it is easy to let things slide after awhile. All it takes is one too many shopping trips or mindlessly putting the laundry away in a haphazard manner, and there you are cluttered and disorganized again. I hate it when that happens!

An easy way to keep from re-cluttering your closets and drawers is by following two simple guidelines:

1. Never buy something new without getting rid of something old
2. Only buy something new if you love it and need it

The first guideline ensures that you will not increase the total number of wardrobe pieces. It does not mean you have to buy something new every time you get rid of something old. It just means your current number of pieces is your *maximum* number of pieces.

A simple way to remind you of this principle for your hanging clothes is to leave just enough hangers in your primary closet for the items you kept after decluttering. Remove all other hangers, possibly storing some in another closet for other uses, such as taking clothing to a consignment store. If you buy something new, you have to take something old off a hanger and sell it, donate it, or toss it.

For folded clothes, if you have designated a drawer for certain categories of clothing, you cannot exceed that capacity. To make room for something new, you have to get rid of something old.

For shoes, you can use the number of available spots on your shoe racks, crates, bins, or shelves to remind you of this principle. If you buy a new pair of shoes, you have to get rid of an old pair. For handbags, the same principle applies. If there is not a designated spot for a new bag to go into, then an old bag has to vacate the spot.

Over time, never buying something new without getting rid of something old will become a habit and you may not even need the visual reminders.

The second guideline is to only buy something new if you love it and need it. This will ensure you build the perfect wardrobe for you. You will no longer settle for "good enough" items. You will not fall for marketing ploys to get you to buy the latest trends regardless of whether they work for you. You will not be fooled into buying something just because it is on sale. (Although you *will* take advantage of sales if you were going to buy the item anyway.) You will not shop out of boredom or to satisfy emotional needs that can be better met in healthier ways. You will not buy clothes that do not fit you, flatter you, or work with your lifestyle. You will only buy what looks and feels good on you. The result? You will end up wearing 100 percent of your clothes...and loving them.

By only buying something if you need it and love it, you may *decrease* your quantity of wardrobe pieces but *increase* the quality. With the *Style & Clothing System*, you will be creating a more versatile, stylish, and personalized wardrobe, so you will not need as many wardrobe pieces. Therefore, you can invest in higher quality for the items you wear the most.

A simple way to remind yourself of the second guideline is to ask these questions whenever you are considering a purchase:

1. Does it fit?
2. Is it comfortable?
3. Do I like how it looks and feels on me?
4. Do I have anything to wear with it?

If your answer to any of the questions is no, then let it go. Wear the clothes, shoes, and handbags you already have until you find exactly what you want.

Eventually, only buying what you love and need will become a habit and you may not even need to ask yourself the questions. They will have become ingrained, and you will have become a stylish woman!

Step 10

Complete Your Style & Clothing Checklist

— — — — — — — — — — — — —

The tenth and final step in the *Style & Clothing System* is to complete a checklist that contains your wardrobe preferences. By gathering all your information together in one place, you will have a handy reference tool to help you create your perfect wardrobe. You can refer to the checklist before shop-ping for clothes, shoes, handbags, jewelry, and other accessories.

The *Style & Clothing Checklist* will also remind you to periodically reassess your closets and drawers to see if anything needs to be altered, repaired, sold, donated, or replaced.

As your body, lifestyle, and tastes change, you can update the checklist to reflect those changes.

> If you completed the CHECKLIST ACTION items as you were reading the guide, you already have most of the information you need.

By completing the following checklist, you will be able to create and maintain a versatile, stylish, person-alized wardrobe. *You can also download a copy of the Style & Clothing Checklist from my website at* http://karalane.com/style-clothing-checklist/.

1. Rank your wardrobe needs based on your lifestyle categories: Ultra Casual, Casual, Dressy Casual, Dressy, and Business. To refresh your memory of the lifestyle category definitions, revisit Step 1.
    a. Lifestyle Need 1:
    b. Lifestyle Need 2:
    c. Lifestyle Need 3:
    d. Lifestyle Need 4:
    e. Lifestyle Need 5:

2. Choose the classics you would most like to have in your wardrobe. To refresh your memory of the classics, revisit Step 2.
    a. Classic 1:
    b. Classic 2:
    c. Classic 3:
    d. Classic 4:
    e. Classic 5:

3. Choose your favorite neutral colors for your clothing. To refresh your memory of neutral colors, revisit Step 3.
    a. Neutral Color 1:
    b. Neutral Color 2:
    c. Neutral Color 3:
    d. Neutral Color 4:
    e. Neutral Color 5:

4. Choose the additional colors you would most like to include in your wardrobe. To refresh your memory of the colors that flatter your skin tone, revisit Step 3.

    a.   Color 1:
    b.   Color 2:
    c.   Color 3:
    d.   Color 4:
    e.   Color 5:

5. Choose your favorite patterns. To refresh your memory of classic patterns, revisit Step 3.

    a.   Pattern 1:
    b.   Pattern 2:
    c.   Pattern 3:
    d.   Pattern 4:
    e.   Pattern 5:

6. Choose the styles and themes that best describe your personal style. To refresh your memory of common styles and themes, revisit Step 3.

    a.   Style 1:
    b.   Style 2:
    c.   Style 3:
    d.   Theme 1:
    e.   Theme 2:
    f.   Theme 3:

7. Choose the clothing styles that flatter your body type and fit your personality. To refresh your memory of styles that flatter each body type, revisit Step 4.
   a. Clothing Style 1:
   b. Clothing Style 2:
   c. Clothing Style 3:

8. Choose the fabrics you prefer most for your wardrobe. To refresh your memory of natural and synthetic fabrics, revisit Step 5.
   a. Fabric 1:
   b. Fabric 2:
   c. Fabric 3:

9. Choose the strategies you would like to use to reduce the quantity of clothing you need. To refresh your memory of the strategies, revisit Step 5.
   a. Strategy 1:
   b. Strategy 2:
   c. Strategy 3:
   d. Strategy 4:
   e. Strategy 5:

186 | THE SMART WOMAN'S GUIDE TO STYLE & CLOTHING

10. Choose your favorite styles of shoes. To refresh your memory of shoe styles, revisit Step 6.
    a. Flats:
    b. Sandals:
    c. Boots:
    d. Pumps:
    e. Sneakers:

11. Choose your favorite styles of handbags. To refresh your memory of handbag styles, revisit Step 6.
    a. Handbag Style 1:
    b. Handbag Style 2:
    c. Handbag Style 3:

12. Choose your favorite styles of jewelry. To refresh your memory of jewelry styles, revisit Step 6.
    a. Necklace Styles:
    b. Earring Styles:
    c. Bracelet Styles:
    d. Ring Styles:

13. Choose your favorite wardrobe brands. To refresh your memory of recommended brands, revisit Step 7.
    a. Clothing Brands:
    b. Shoe Brands:
    c. Handbag Brands:
    d. Jewelry Brands:

14. Choose your favorite stores. To refresh your memory of recommended stores, revisit Step 7.

     a.   Store 1:
     b.   Store 2:
     c.   Store 3:
     d.   Store 4:
     e.   Store 5:

15. Choose your favorite color combinations. To refresh your memory of colors that combine well, revisit Step 8.

     a.   Color Combo 1:
     b.   Color Combo 2:
     c.   Color Combo 3:
     d.   Color Combo 4:
     e.   Color Combo 5:

16. Choose your favorite style resources. To refresh your memory of recommended style resources, revisit Step 8.

     a.   Style Resource 1:
     b.   Style Resource 2:
     c.   Style Resource 3:
     d.   Style Resource 4:
     e.   Style Resource 5:

17. Schedule your next decluttering and organizing session. To refresh your memory on how best to declutter and organize, revisit Step 9.

    a. Date of your next decluttering and organizing sessions:

    b. Where you will have clothes altered or repaired:

    c. Where you will have shoes & handbags altered or repaired:

    d. Where you will sell items you no longer want:

    e. Where you will donate items you no longer want:

18. Note any rules you choose to follow when you shop for clothing. Example 1: Only buy straight-leg, mid-rise jeans. Example 2: Stick to 3 heel heights for shoes: flat, 1-inch, and 3-inches. Example 3: Do not buy any more black pants…have too many already.

    a. Rule 1:

    b. Rule 2:

    c. Rule 3:

    d. Rule 4:

    e. Rule 5:

19. Choose the wardrobe pieces you would like to buy next. Be as specific as possible. Example: *Black, mid-length trench coat.*
    a.   Wardrobe Piece 1:
    b.   Wardrobe Piece 2:
    c.   Wardrobe Piece 3:
    d.   Wardrobe Piece 4:
    e.   Wardrobe Piece 5.

20. Questions to ask yourself before you buy a new item for your wardrobe:
    a.   Do I love it? *Yes = You love how it looks and feels on you*
    b.   Do I need it? *Yes = It fits your life-style & you have something to wear with it*

The purpose of the *Style & Clothing Checklist* is to help you create a wardrobe you will love and wear. It is a reminder of what *you* have chosen for *your* wardrobe. It will keep you focused on buying only what you love and need.

Keep a copy of the checklist in your handbag or on your smartphone. When you are shopping (or thinking of going shopping), read your checklist first. It will help you to avoid impulse buying.

You may also want to keep a copy of your checklist on your computer. When you are shopping online, call up your checklist and read it before you click on the order button.

If you succumb to temptation and impulsively buy something online or off…well, that just proves you are human. Go ahead and run it through the checklist after the fact. If it passes muster, keep it. If not, return it. No harm, no foul.

Conclusion

‒ ‒ ‒ ‒ ‒ ‒ ‒ ‒ ‒

My goal in writing the *Style & Clothing System* was to provide you with the expertise to create your own versatile, stylish, personalized wardrobe. Beyond providing you with a detailed clothing system, my intention was to encourage you to be mindful about your wardrobe choices. Think before you buy, and you will buy more things that make you look and feel good.

When I have mentioned wearing what makes you feel good throughout this guide, you may have thought I was referring to your wardrobe items. I was, but I was also referring to how your buying behavior makes you feel. When you impulsively buy something you do not really want or need, the short-term gain of getting something new is outweighed by long-term losses: wasted money, cluttered closets, and a mediocre wardrobe. When you instead choose your wardrobe thoughtfully, the short-term loss of instant gratification is more than offset by long-term gains: pride for spending money wisely, serenity from having an organized closet, increased confidence in your style, and a beautiful look-good, feel-good wardrobe.

Viktor Frankl, author of *Man's Search for Meaning*, said, "Between stimulus and response, there is a space. In that space is our power to choose our response. In our response lies our growth and our freedom." While he was talking about far bigger things than clothing, the same advice applies. The stimulus to buy clothing could be something you see. Something in a store, in a magazine, or on a website, may catch your eye. It could also be something you feel. The urge to shop can arise out of boredom, loneliness, a desire to socialize, to avoid doing something else, or any reason other than need. Retail therapy can be a stress-reliever, but so can meditation, getting out in nature, and spending time with family and friends. If you pause between stimulus (the desire to shop) and response (actually purchasing something), you will give yourself time to make better choices. When something triggers the urge to shop – just pause, pull out your *Style & Clothing Checklist*, and then decide whether you really want to buy more stuff.

Every day, we are bombarded with marketing messages telling us to buy more stuff. The late comedian George Carlin said, "A house is just a place to keep your stuff while you go out and get more stuff." For many people, all their stuff will not even fit in their homes anymore. According to the Self Storage Association, Americans spend $24 billion each year to store their stuff. That is a lot of stuff.

If having all that stuff made us happy, I would be all for it. But studies show that all our new stuff does not make us happier. According to a *Wall Street Journal* article by Andrew Blackman, giving money away makes us happier than spending it on ourselves. When we do spend money on ourselves, we tend to be happier when the money is spent on experiences like travel, rather than on material things. Cornell University psychology professor Thomas Gilovich says we adapt to our material goods, and take them for granted after the initial pleasure. With experiences, the memories can last a lifetime.

If we shopped less frequently but more thoughtfully, we could look great while saving time and money, simplifying our lives, and increasing our happiness. We would also free up resources for the things that matter most to us.

If your shopping behavior is sometimes driven by a desire to please or impress others, ask yourself who you are trying to impress.

Sometimes we dress to impress our friends. If they have the latest designer clothes, shoes, handbags, or jewelry, we want them, too. It feels good when someone says, "I love your new shoes!" Or, "Is that a new handbag? I love it!" But it can also become addictive. After all, the first time people see your new wardrobe piece, you will get lots of compliments. But once they've seen it, they've seen it. Now you have to go get something else new to get your compliment fix. Better to impress them with your kindness and wit...they are free and last longer!

Sometimes we dress to impress the guys. But surprisingly, while dressing sexy may catch a guy's attention, it will not hold it for long. According to James Sama, a successful blogger, speaker, and motivator, the seven things men think make a woman sexy are confidence, ambition, passion, kindness, honesty, class, and intelligence. Similarly, an article by Brooke Blue in *Shape Magazine*, stated that what men find most attractive about women is kindness, honesty, independence, a positive personality, and having quirky interests. Hmmm, not one mention about clothes, shoes, handbags, or jewelry.

If you are going to dress to impress someone, dress to impress yourself. Wear what makes you feel your best. The irony is that we are more likely to impress other people when we are not trying. When we are just being ourselves, we are more relaxed and confident. We smile more. As a result, we are more attractive. Go figure.

A wise approach when considering a new piece for your wardrobe is to remember the tale of *The Emperor's New Clothes* by Hans Christian Andersen. In this children's story, two swindlers tell the emperor and the townspeople that they have a magical cloth that can only be seen by wise and worthy people. They claim that it is the finest cloth in the land, but it is invisible to people who are stupid. The emperor is a vain man who spends all his money on clothing, so he tells the fraudulent weavers to create a set of clothes for him. They pretend to weave the suit and he pretends he can see it, because he does not want to be thought a fool. He lets the weavers dress him in the new suit and parades around town in his underwear. The townspeople cannot see the clothes, but out of fear of looking stupid, they pretend to admire them anyway. Finally, a child points out the truth: the emperor has no clothes.

The moral of the story is to think for yourself. Trust what you believe and what you see with your own eyes. Just because everyone else is raving about a designer brand or the latest trend does not mean you have to follow the crowd. Choose the wardrobe pieces that work best for you.

There are just two questions you need to ask yourself when you are considering adding a piece to your wardrobe:

- Do you love it?
- Do you need it?

These same two questions are the last item on the *Style & Clothing Checklist*. They tell you everything you need to know. The purpose of this book has been to help you answer those two questions.

Do you love it? The answer is either yes or no. You always know the answer to that question, but you may not have always known why. Now you do. If you do not instinctively love a wardrobe piece, it is probably for one of the reasons we have discussed. The pants do not fit. The shoes are not comfortable. The handbag looks cheap. The jewelry is not your style. The colors of the blouse and skirt clash. The dress does not flatter your body shape. The top does not flatter your skin tone. The shoes are not right for the pants. And so on. The bottom line is you are only going to love it if it looks and feels good on you.

Before you buy something for your wardrobe, always ask yourself if you love it. No buts. If you say it is a little too tight, *but* you love the color…then you do not love it. Put it back. If you bought something and love how it fits, *but* it is not your style…then you do not love it. Return it. Hold out for something you really love, not something you have to rationalize your way into buying or keeping.

To become more stylish, also ask yourself why you love something or why you do not love it. You will learn a lot by your answers, which you can then use to guide future purchases.

Do you need it? Normally, I would agree with the Beatles that "all you need is love." But not in this case. You also have to ask yourself whether you need it. If you already own it, by all means, keep it. But if you are thinking of buying something new, consider your needs as well as your wants.

This question is harder to answer than the first one. You instinctively know if you love something or not. Need is harder to pin down. You can make the question easier to answer by considering what we have discussed in this guide. For example…

Does it fit your lifestyle? Even if it is the most beautiful cocktail dress you have ever seen in your entire life, you clearly do not need it if you rarely go to cocktail parties.

Do you have anything to wear with it? Even if you love those bright green pants, you will not be able to wear them if your closet it full of olive, brown, and cream tops. Not to be a killjoy, but you do not need those pants.

Do you already have too many of the same thing? Imelda Marcos was rumored to have over 3,000 pairs of shoes. I would argue that no matter how much she loved her shoes, she did not need another pair.

I would also encourage you to consider your physical space. If your closets and drawers are already cluttered, you probably do not need anything else right now.

Beyond that, we all have to determine whether we "need" an item based on our own preferences and personal circumstances.

Of course, rules are made to be broken. If you see something and think you really, really, really love it, then wait a few days to see if you still feel the same way. If you still love it and it fits within your budget, go for it. Just remember to get rid of something else so you will not clutter up your closet.

Finally, remember to be patient when creating your new wardrobe. Rome wasn't built in a day, and your perfect wardrobe won't be either. No rush. While you are waiting to find those perfect pieces, work on the other things that affect how you look in your clothes and shoes. Cleaning, polishing, and taking care of your current wardrobe pieces will make them look better. Putting together different pieces, rather than wearing the same things together all the time, will increase your number of outfits. Taking better care of your body will make you look better in your clothes. Moisturizing and grooming your feet will make them look better in your sandals. Working on your posture will improve your looks and your health. Loving and accepting yourself will make you happier, more confident, and more attractive...no matter what you are wearing.

How you use the *Style & Clothing System* is up to you. Go as minimalist or maximalist as you wish. If you are happy, I am happy. Because this guide is not really about the clothes. It is about giving you the tools to look like the amazing woman you are, so you can get on with your life and not worry about what to wear. The system takes an up-front investment of time and effort, but it will ultimately give you the freedom to focus on more important things. So go on, change the world...and look good doing it!

Note from the Author

I hope you enjoyed reading *The Smart Woman's Guide to Style & Clothing* as much as I enjoyed writing it for you.

If you found the book helpful, please spread the word and consider posting a review on Amazon or on the site where you purchased the book. Other readers will appreciate it, and so will I.

Please contact me at kara@karalane.com if you have comments, questions, or something you would like me to cover in future editions.

You can also find me here:

Twitter (@AuthorKaraLane)

Pinterest (www.pinterest.com/karadlane)

My website (www.karalane.com)

If you are new to my writing, please check out my other books on Amazon:

From Photographer to Gallery Artist
The Complete Guide to Finding Gallery Representation for Your Fine Art Photography

Simoni's Gift
A Story about Your Purpose in Life

Wake Up to Powerful Living
12 Principles to Transform Your Life!

BONUS MATERIAL: Interested in a behind-the-scenes look at the making of *The Smart Woman's Guide to Style & Clothing*? Then check out the appendix that follows. You will discover how the book was written, published, and marketed, as well as how the images were created.

APPENDIX

Behind the Scenes of *The Smart Woman's Guide to Style & Clothing*

W hen I wrote my first book, I was completely clueless. I thought I had a "book in me" and that it would practically write itself. Turns out, it doesn't work that way. Publishing a book is a lengthy process. So far, I have spent over 600 hours on

The Smart Woman's Guide to Style & Clothing. That is just the cumulative time as I write these words. I will spend hundreds of hours more publishing the book and marketing it. If you have ever wanted to publish a book, read on...

Publishing a book is a three-part process:
• Writing
• Publishing
• Marketing

Writing

The writing phase begins with choosing a topic. I chose the topic for this book for personal reasons. I wanted a style and clothing system, and I could not find one. I did some research to find out if others were interested in the topic. They were.

I conducted online and offline research to find out everything I could about style and clothing. I read style books, magazines, articles, and blogs. I used my local library's databases to conduct additional research. Then I interviewed some experts and requested quotes from others. Additionally, I went to several malls and consignment shops to watch women shop. (And I can tell you from my people watching, we women do like to impulse shop...big time.) Finally, I read the reviews of other style books to see what reviewers liked and disliked.

When I felt I had done enough research, I sat down to analyze and organize the information I had gathered. All along, I had been recording my observations, ideas, thoughts, and plans in a notebook, so I went over those notes as well.

I then began to formulate the central message of the book. Who was I writing for? What did I want to say? How did I want to organize the book? I did not want to just do a data dump...you could get that from a Google search. I wanted to put together a step-by-step process to make it easier for you to create your ideal wardrobe.

Once I was clear about whom I was writing for and what I wanted to say, I outlined the book. I used index cards, because they make it easier to reorganize sections. On each index card, I wrote a main point with subpoints underneath it. Eventually, I had one master index card for each chapter of the book: the introduction, each of the steps (which became chapters), the conclusion, the front matter (like the copyright page), and the back matter (like this appendix).

Finally, I started writing...and writing...and writing. More accurately, I began typing...and typing...and typing. This part took months...and months...and months.

I did four major drafts. In the first draft, I just tried to get all my thoughts down for each step of the system. I did not stop to edit, conduct additional research, or worry about word choice. I just made notes in red of anything I needed to address later. The first draft is never pretty, and this one was no exception.

In the second draft, I focused on making sure my message was clear. This is where I began editing the content. I added words, deleted words, and moved things around. I also did some additional research and fact checking.

In the third draft, I did the final editing for spelling, grammar, punctuation, consistency, flow, etc. This is the draft where I polished my writing to make it as clear, concise, and complete as possible.

Then I turned the book over to beta readers. A beta reader is not the same as an editor or proofreader. Beta readers read the manuscript and give you their feedback. They tell you what they liked, disliked, found confusing, found boring, etc.

In the fourth draft, I incorporated feedback from my beta readers. Then I read the entire manuscript one more time and made my final edits.

That is a quick overview of the writing phase. I should mention that this is the process for a nonfiction book. I have written fiction as well, which follows a different process.

Publishing

The publishing phase comes next. While writing is about the content, publishing is about turning the manuscript into a physical or digital book. It is how the book looks and is made.

In this phase, I finalized the title and cover design. Both are key to creating a good first impression with readers.

The title for a nonfiction book must make the subject of the book clear. A book with a clever title that does not clearly identify the topic will not be found via search. People search on key words, so the title must include the types of words for which they will be searching. That is why I used key words like "style," "clothing," "guide," "step-by-step," and "wardrobe" in my title and subtitle.

I narrowed down my title and subtitle options to my three favorites and then took a poll to see which title people liked best. That is how I arrived at the title, *The Smart Woman's Guide to Style & Clothing: A Step-By-Step Process for Creating the Perfect Wardrobe.*

The cover is also very important, because it is the first thing people see when they look at a book. It needs to be eye-catching and look professional. If you just use a generic template with a stock photo, the result will not be impressive. With my first two books, I used stock photos. With this book and the one before it, I worked with award-winning fine art photographer Tenna Merchent to create the cover image.

Interior formatting must also be done during the publishing process. The look and design of the interior pages affects the ease of reading. Although eBooks are easier to format than print books, you still must ensure bullet points, numbered lists, page breaks, images, links, the table of contents, etc. will display properly regardless of what type of device the reader is using... Kindle, iPad, Nook, etc.

Interior formatting for print books is even more difficult if you want a professional-looking book. In addition to the same issues as eBooks, you have to address issues like proper hyphenation and pagination. For example, the introduction and first chapter should always start on the right-hand page. Also, even-numbered pages should be on the left and odd-numbered pages on the right. There are additional issues related to strange-sounding things like gutter space, bleed, DPI, and grayscale that a good formatter will understand. As a reader, you do not have to know what they are, but they affect whether the reading experience is good or bad.

A related step in the publishing process is to choose publishing formats and platforms. For *The Smart Woman's Guide to Style & Clothing*, I chose to publish the paperback format through the CreateSpace platform and the eBook format through the Kindle Direct Publishing platform. Both are part of Amazon.

For a paperback, you have to make decisions regarding the physical book, such as what trim size to use. Trim size refers to the size of the page. I chose a standard trim size for this book because it allows me to distribute the book more widely, such as through Barnes & Noble and other booksellers in addition to Amazon.

You also have to choose the paper color for paperbacks. This book has images and images display better on white paper, so that is what I used. For books that are just text, I have sometimes used cream paper, which some readers feel is easier on the eyes.

For an eBook, you have to know what kind of file format will be used. Amazon Kindle uses .mobi files, but Apple iBooks and most other platforms use .epub files. Since I planned to go with Kindle initially, I had to make sure all their technical specifications would be met before uploading my cover image and book.

The publishing phase requires making decisions regarding things like which book categories and keywords to use, what text to include on the back cover, what to put on the copyright page, where to sell the book (distribution channels and countries), how to price the book, etc.

Finally, publishing requires you to make choices regarding the ISBN and LCCN numbers. The ISBN is the International Standard Book Number, and it is how publishers, booksellers, and libraries identify the book. The LCCN is the Library of Congress Control Number and it is used by libraries for cataloging the book. Making good decisions regarding these items protects the rights of authors and makes it easier for readers to find our books.

Marketing

Marketing is the final phase of the book-publishing process. When I published my first book, I naively assumed my job was just to do my best to write a good book. After that, I figured I would just put it on Amazon and readers would find it. Oh, if that were only true!

Amazon carries millions of book titles. According to *TechCrunch*, there is a new book published on Amazon every 5 minutes or less. Some of the books are great...some, not so much. The problem is that even good books by unknown authors can get lost in the shuffle.

If you are a famous author (like J.K. Rowling or Dan Brown), or a celebrity author (whose books are often written by a ghostwriter), people will specifically search for your books. However, lesser-known authors often rely on readers finding them through search. Bestselling books will be at the top of the list for any searches, so an unknown author's book could end up on page 20 of search results. No one ever looks that far, which means the book will probably not be discovered that way.

That is where marketing comes in. Marketing should ideally start before you even write the book. First, you have to figure out who is the audience for your type of book. (Hint: the correct answer is never "everyone.") Second, you have to create a great book that informs, entertains, and inspires your readers. Third, you have to find out how to reach your readers. They must discover your book before they can buy it. Fourth, you have to make the sale. Your title, cover, and book description must intrigue them enough to want to purchase your book.

Marketing effectively requires an author to build an audience for their books, also known as building a platform in the publishing world. This can take awhile. I did no marketing with my first book and very little with my second. Not surprisingly, they did not sell well.

The first time I actively marketed a book was with my third book, *From Photographer to Gallery Artist*. I contacted a local paper and they interviewed me. I was a guest on a popular photography podcast. I wrote articles for LinkedIn. I contacted the editor of a best-selling photography reference book and ended up doing a few guest posts for them, as well as writing an article that will appear in the 2017 edition of their annual publication. Because of my marketing efforts, my last book has sold more than the first two books combined. I just have to continue to promote it to the right audience to increase the momentum.

There are many different ways to market a book depending on the type of book, the market for the book, the author's or publisher's budget, the amount of time available to promote the book, the size of the author's platform, etc.

For *The Smart Woman's Guide to Style & Clothing*, some of the things I will do to market my book include:

- Promoting the book on my website (www.karalane.com)
- Holding a book giveaway on Goodreads (a social media site for readers)
- Reaching out to readers on Twitter, Pinterest, LinkedIn, etc.
- Doing guest posts on sites where my prospective readers hang out
- Contacting the media to offer information about my book's topic
- Attending writers workshops where I will meet others in the publishing world

- Reaching out to fans and influencers interested in the topic of my book

So there you have it! A condensed version of what goes into writing, publishing, and marketing a book.

Although I have created a system for publishing books, every book is different. For instance, one thing that was different for *The Smart Woman's Guide to Style & Clothing* was that I included images in a book for the first time. Speaking of which...

Images

Have you ever wondered why so many style books do not include images? Even best-selling style books often contain illustrations, but no photos. I used to think a style book with no photos of clothes was like a cookbook with no photos of recipes.

Now, I get it. It is very expensive to publish a paperback or hardcover book with images, especially if the images are in color. If you have a printer at home, you know printer ink is not cheap.

I discovered that if I wanted color images in the paperback format of this book, it would triple my publishing costs. The problem is that readers might not be willing to pay three times more for the book just to get color images. Would you have paid three times more for color images?

If the cost to print each book triples, but the price does not go up, there is no profit left for the author. The printer will be paid, the book retailer will be paid, the people hired to help with the book (like editors, cover designers, and interior formatters) will be paid, but there will be nothing left over. The author would then be working for free. Can you imagine working for six months to a year or longer and not being paid? Perish the thought!

This is an even bigger issue for indie authors, who use print on demand technology rather than offset printing. Traditional publishers use offset printing because they can print off a large number of copies at a time, which reduces the cost per book. Indie authors cannot afford to do this, so their books are just printed as customers order them. In other words, they are printed on demand, one at a time.

I still thought you would prefer images in a style book, so I found a work-around. I put color images in my eBook, but printed the paperback with black and white images. One benefit of the black and white images is that you can substitute your color choices for the actual colors of the wardrobe pieces. If you would like to see the images in color, you can find them on my website on this post: http://karalane.com/images-smart-womans-guide-style-clothing-kara-lane/.

The cost of printing is not the only reason many

style books do not include images. Additional time, money, and effort are needed for other reasons as well. For instance, unless you are a professional photographer, you have to hire someone to capture the images for the book. You also have to obtain the clothing for the images.

To create the images for *The Smart Woman's Guide to Style & Clothing*, I mainly used my own clothes. I borrowed a couple of things and bought a few others, but most of the clothes came from my closet. It would have been cost-prohibitive if I had needed to purchase everything.

Including images is also a lot more work. Clothing has to be posed. Unlike models who can pose themselves, clothes just sit there until you arrange them.

Formatting is also more difficult with images. Unless you have the appropriate software and technical expertise, you will probably have to outsource the interior formatting of books with images. Sophia Wiedeman did the interior formatting for this book.

To compose the images inside *The Smart Woman's Guide to Style & Clothing*, I threw a white comforter over our guest room bed to imitate the white studio where we would be shooting the final images. I arranged different outfits on the bed until I liked the result. Then I climbed up on a step stool and took pictures of the outfits with my iPhone. This allowed me to capture how

I had arranged the clothing so I could do it again in the studio. The outfits were shot on a white seamless background in photographer Tenna Merchent's studio.

After the first photo shoot at the studio, it occurred to me that there was an important issue that had to be addressed. I remembered from my brief modeling stint that you cannot display a logo or label without authorization. I once showed up wearing an Adidas top for a commercial where I was going to be rollerblading. The wardrobe people had to cover up the Adidas logo with black tape.

Since every article of clothing, pair of shoes, and handbag has labels and logos, we had a problem. To avoid legal issues, I had to request that the photographer edit out all the labels and logos in Photoshop. Thank you, Tenna!

Fortunately, I was better prepared for the second shoot. I studied style magazines and saw that they often turn shoes on their sides in their images. That hides the logos inside the shoes. Brilliant! For the second shoot, I turned the shoes sideways and found creative ways to hide labels in clothing so there would be fewer logos and labels that needed to be edited out. (So if you are paying close attention to the images in *The Smart Woman's Guide to Style & Clothing*, you can probably tell which images were taken at the first shoot and which were taken at the second!)

At the third shoot, we did the cover image. To compose the cover image, I borrowed a clothing rack from a friend and then experimented with different wardrobe pieces and props in my kitchen. Once I found the look I liked, I took pictures on my iPhone, so I could recreate the cover scene when we shot the cover for real. We scoped out a location, and the photographer made sure the lighting and everything else was good to go. Then she captured the images and applied a filter to give the cover the look of an oil painting.

That's all folks! I hope you enjoyed the peek behind the curtain to see how a book is published. If you decide to write and publish a book, I am cheering for you all the way! It is a lot of work, but it gives you a tremendous sense of accomplishment when the book is...finally... published.

All the best,

Kara Lane

Acknowledgements

I would like to thank everyone who contributed to the making of *The Smart Woman's Guide to Style & Clothing*.

Thanks to Tenna Merchent for photographing and editing the images used in the book and on the cover.

Thanks to Sophia Wiedeman for interior formatting and cover design.

Thanks to everyone else who provided quotes, helpful feedback, or beta reading services:

- Debbie Mikulla – Owner of *Closet Control* & Consultant for *Etcetera*
- Grasie Mercedes – Actress and Fashion Blogger for *Style Me Grasie*
- Jenni Meyers – Owner of the *Beauty + Grace* Clothing Store
- Jessica Filippi – Freelance Writer and Editor
- Jessica Landez – Owner of *BluePeppermint Boutique*
- Marti Gordon – Personal Stylist, *The Fifth Avenue Club* at Saks Fifth Avenue

- Sara Donaldson – Fashion Blogger for *Harper & Harley*
- Susan Caito – Privacy Manager and Style Aficionado
- Valerie Porter – Writer, Editor, Proofreader, and Book Reviewer

Last but never least, I want to thank my husband, Rick. While he prefers reading thrillers and books on coaching, success, athletics, and the Navy SEALs, he still helped me edit this style guide…and all the books that came before it. He makes me a better writer, and a better person. Thank you, Babe.

Made in the USA
Columbia, SC
14 August 2017